Gao Jun and Du Min

**Mastering DeepSeek in 7 Days**

## Also of Interest

*Mastering ChatGPT.*
*Prompts and Beyond*
George Grätzer, 2025
ISBN 978-3-11-171050-1, e-ISBN (PDF) 978-3-11-171080-8,
e-ISBN (EPUB) 978-3-11-171089-1

*Math Optimization for Artificial Intelligence.*
*Heuristic and Metaheuristic Methods for Robotics and Machine Learning*
Umesh Kumar Lilhore, Vishal Dutt, T. Ananth Kumar, Martin Margala,
Kaamran Raahemifar (Eds.), 2025
ISBN 978-3-11-143605-0, e-ISBN (PDF) 978-3-11-143618-0,
e-ISBN (EPUB) 978-3-11-143624-1

*Generative AI for Software Development.*
*Code Generation, Error Detection, Software Testing*
Seifedine Kadry and Balasubramaniam S (Eds.), 2025
ISBN 978-3-11-167772-9, e-ISBN (PDF) 978-3-11-167779-8,
e-ISBN (EPUB) 978-3-11-167815-3

*Intelligent Educational Robots.*
*Toward Personalized Learning Environments*
Stamatios Papadakis and Georgios Lampropoulos (Eds.), 2025
ISBN 978-3-11-135206-0, e-ISBN (PDF) 978-3-11-135269-5,
e-ISBN (EPUB) 978-3-11-135296-1

Gao Jun and Du Min

# Mastering DeepSeek in 7 Days

Core Architecture, Prompt Engineering, Prompt Optimization

DE GRUYTER

**Authors**
**Gao Jun**
Founder of Singapore-Based AI Company
Technology Cloud PTE. LTD (ai.y.org.cn)
Executive President of the Shaanxi Chamber of Commerce
Guangdong
China

**Du Min**
University Lecturer Specializing in AI
Council Member of the Higher Education
Technology Committee Under the
Guangxi Higher Education Association
Guangxi
China

Translated by MingZhe.
English edition is coordinated with KALIMA Culture & Media (Beijing).

ISBN 978-3-11-914389-9
ISBN 978-3-11-221818-1 (PDF)
ISBN 978-3-11-221846-4 (EPUB)
DOI https://doi.org/10.1515/9783112218181

Library of Congress Control Number: 2026933228

Bibliographic information published by the Deutsche Nationalbibliothek
The Deutsche Nationalbibliothek lists this publication in the Deutsche Nationalbibliografie; detailed bibliographic data are available on the Internet at http://dnb.dnb.de.



De Gruyter and Walter de Gruyter GmbH are part of De Gruyter Brill.
www.degruyterbrill.com

Questions about General Product Safety Regulation:
productsafety@degruyterbrill.com

Cover illustration: Philip Thurston/E+/Getty Images

# Preface

In this era of rapid technological transformation, as a Chinese student studying abroad, I have personally witnessed the sweeping and disruptive power of the global tech revolution. At the same time, I have deeply felt the surging momentum of my homeland striving for self-reliance and catching up in the field of artificial intelligence (AI). Looking back, from the early days of studying overseas, to being immersed in the high-tech hubs of Silicon Valley and Europe, and later exploring real-world AI applications back in China, I have been consistently inspired by the immense charm of technology and the innovative spirit of researchers. It was through this invaluable journey that a compelling idea was born: to integrate advanced international concepts with domestic practical strengths, and to help more people understand and master the core technologies of AI – so they can better embrace the challenges and opportunities of the digital era.

This book, *DeepSeek Mastery: From Beginner to Expert in 7 Days*, was conceived in this very context. Using the cutting-edge Chinese AI large model DeepSeek as its entry point, this book systematically covers everything from basic operations and prompt engineering to industry-level applications. It features nearly 200 practical examples and over 140 optimization strategies, aiming to translate complex technical principles into a practical guide that is accessible and actionable for everyone. Valley and beyond, while also integrating the unique practices arising from China's strategy of achieving high-level technological self-reliance. Each exchange and discussion with experts and technical teams deepened my understanding and technical teams deepened my understanding of intelligent and digital transformation.

The creation of this book has been a journey of relearning and breakthrough. It not only documents my observations of frontier technologies during my time abroad but also gathers my practical insights after returning to China. This book balances rigorous theoretical explanation with intuitive demonstrations of real operations. It aims to serve as a forward-looking, practical guide for researchers, technical experts, and general users alike. More than a personal reflection of growth, this book is a gift to the times and to all technology enthusiasts. I firmly believe that in today's advancing wave of digitalization, every reader passionate about technology can draw inspiration from it, quickly enhance their skills, and find their place in the AI revolution – contributing to social progress and industrial upgrading.

May this book serve as a guiding light on your journey into AI, illuminating the path ahead, and empowering all of us to welcome a smarter and better future together.

February 2025

 | https://doi.org/10.1515/9783112218181-202

# Foreword

The technological revolution of the new era is sweeping the globe at an unprecedented pace, with artificial intelligence (AI) as the core engine driving this wave, quietly transforming our production models and ways of life. Under the national strategy of "high-level self-reliance and self-strengthening in science and technology," China has made remarkable progress in the field of AI, demonstrating robust innovative vitality – from foundational algorithms to the deep integration of various application scenarios. Meanwhile, overseas models driven by open collaboration and venture capital continue to redefine perceptions of technological boundaries. It is precisely this complementary dynamic between East and West, where strengths mutually reinforce each other, that provides rich theoretical foundations and practical material for the creation of this book.

Centered on the cutting-edge domestic AI model DeepSeek, this book offers a comprehensive analysis of its architectural principles, operational mechanisms, and real-world applications. From the most basic account registration and interface navigation to the intricate construction of prompt engineering, and further to applications across diverse fields such as smart office work, family education, daily life, content creation, financial decision-making, and cross-platform integration, this book not only details every step of technical implementation but also showcases how to translate theory into actionable solutions through nearly 200 examples and numerous optimization strategies. Suitable for beginners seeking a quick start, it also serves as an in-depth guide for professionals.

 | https://doi.org/10.1515/9783112218181-203

# Foreword

During the drafting process, we strived to present a novel intelligent application system that combines a global perspective with deep-rooted local practices. This approach not only enables readers to grasp global AI trends but also equips them with hands-on experience, rapidly enhancing their application capabilities and providing strong support for seizing opportunities in the digital transformation of individuals and enterprises alike.

In summary, this book is not merely a detailed technical manual but also a practical guide that documents epochal changes and witnesses technological progress. It helps readers fully understand the intrinsic logic and application techniques of DeepSeek while offering valuable insights for addressing the multifaceted challenges of future intelligent and digital development. We hope that readers will not only acquire practical skills but also gain a clear view of the new trends in global technological competition, collectively propelling China toward higher levels of innovation and development in the intelligent revolution.

 | https://doi.org/10.1515/9783112218181-204

# Contents

# Chapter 1
# Core Architecture, Working Principles, and Applications of DeepSeek

DeepSeek is one of China's leading large-scale artificial intelligence (AI) models, specifically engineered for natural language processing (NLP), text generation, intelligent Q&A, and code generation in Chinese contexts. This chapter details DeepSeek's core architecture, operational principles, and the practical implementation of its modules across real-world applications. Through structured organization, standardized terminology, and abundant examples, it equips readers to master DeepSeek's underlying logic, establishing a robust foundation for subsequent application and optimization techniques.

## 1.1 DeepSeek Core Architecture and Operational Principles

DeepSeek's architecture builds upon the mainstream transformer model, integrating advantages from massive-scale pretraining and multitask learning. Its framework comprises the following key modules.

### 1.1.1 Data Input and Preprocessing Module (Example: Processing Meeting Minutes Data)

DeepSeek can accept various forms of user input, such as text, speech, or images. The data input module is responsible for converting these raw inputs into a standardized format. For text inputs, the module automatically cleans the data by removing noise and special characters. For voice inputs, it utilizes advanced speech recognition technology to convert audio into text. For image inputs, it employs image recognition algorithms to extract key information. For instance, when a user submits meeting minutes as text input, the system automatically identifies and extracts critical sections, removes extraneous symbols, and ensures clean data with unified formatting for subsequent processing:

 | https://doi.org/10.1515/9783112218181-001

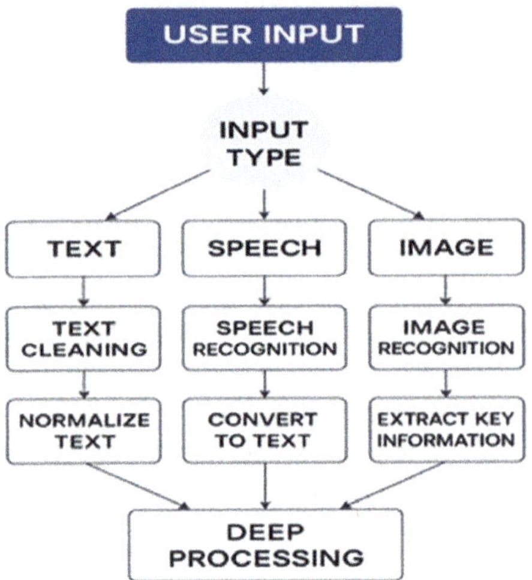


### 1.1.2 Natural Language Understanding and Semantic Parsing Module (Example: Command Parsing)

This module serves as a core cognitive engine of DeepSeek, employing advanced NLP technology to perform semantic parsing of input texts and accurately interpret user intent. Built on pretrained models, it identifies keywords, phrases, and syntactic structures to extract essential information:

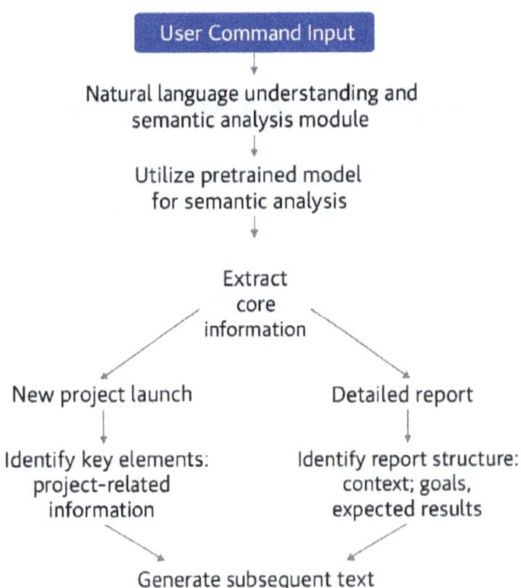

### 1.1.3 Text Generation Module (Example: Code Auto-Generation)

Leveraging the transformer architecture and large-scale pretraining techniques, DeepSeek can generate high-quality text based on parsing results. This module supports multitask generation, including long-form reports, concise answers, code snippets, and more, while ensuring logical coherence and linguistic accuracy in its outputs. For example, when generating code, a user may input: “please write Python code to calculate the average of a list.” The system will automatically produce well-commented code. Similarly, when generating a work report, the user can enter relevant instructions, and the system will generate a well-structured, data-supported report draft (note: all generative content and diagrams in this book must be output in HTML format, and users should be aware of this during use):

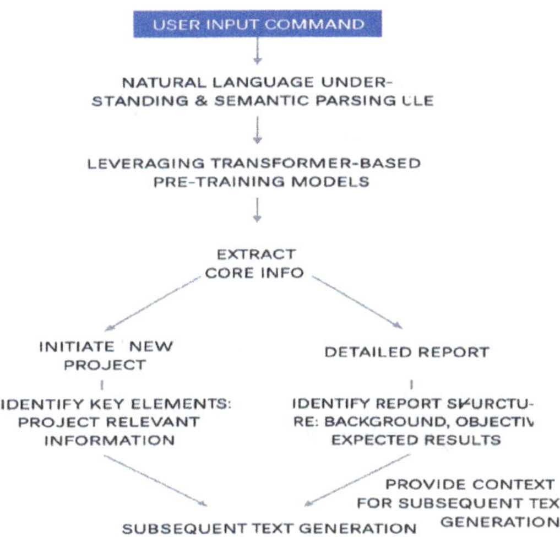


### 1.1.4 Feedback and Iterative Optimization Module (Example: Content Refinement via User Adjustment)

To ensure output quality and precision, DeepSeek employs a structured feedback mechanism. Users can evaluate and refine initially generated content, enabling the system to dynamically adjust generation strategies through multiple optimization iterations until meeting user expectations:

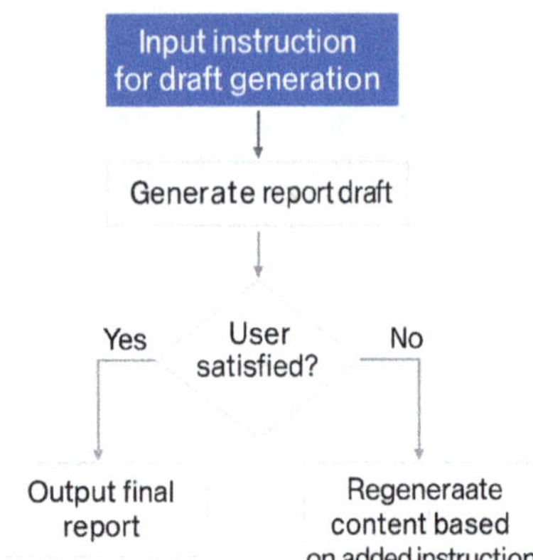


## 1.2 DeepSeek Real-World Application

DeepSeek's core architecture endows it with distinctive capabilities in the following common tasks.

### 1.2.1 Text Generation (Example: Official Document Drafting and Academic Summarization)

Application example: Drafting work reports, abstracts for academic papers, etc.

Operation detailed steps: User provides detailed instructions → system analyzes and generates initial draft → user refines → outputs polished text.

### 1.2.2 Intelligent Q&A (Example: Technical Support and Business Consulting)

Application example: Answering business inquiries, technical questions, etc.

Operation detailed steps: User poses specific question → system interprets the context → generates concise response → user may ask follow-up questions for additional details.

### 1.2.3 Code Generation (Example: Python Code Auto-Generation)

Application example: Assisting programming and generating debugging code.

Operation detailed steps: The user inputs the command "please generate Python code to calculate the average" → the system outputs a commented code snippet → the user debugs, modifies, and applies it directly.

# Chapter 2
# Getting Started with DeepSeek

This chapter guides readers in mastering DeepSeek's basic operations from scratch. By detailing the registration process, interface navigation, text generation, and interactive feedback mechanisms, readers will quickly familiarize themselves with this leading Chinese large language model tool, laying a solid foundation for future advanced applications.

## 2.1 Registration and Account Management

### 2.1.1 Account Registration Process

To use DeepSeek, registration is required via the official website or mobile app. Users must provide a valid email address or phone number and set a secure password. An automated system will send a verification code for identity authentication:

(1) Visit the DeepSeek official website or download the DeepSeek mobile app:

(2) For first-time registration, enter your email address or phone number:

 | https://doi.org/10.1515/9783112218181-002

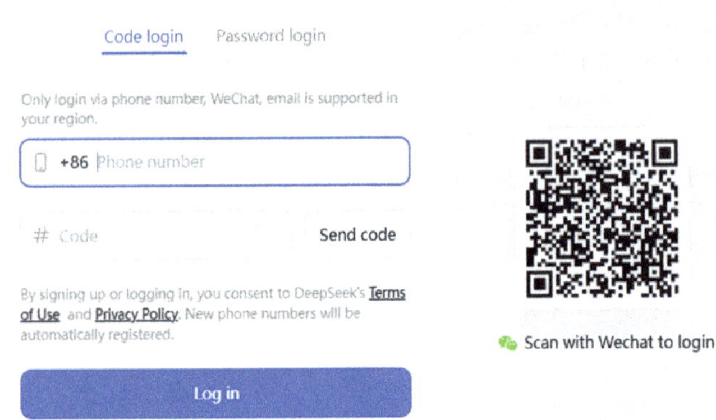


(3) Input the received verification code in the designated field to complete authentication.
(4) After successful registration, log in as prompted and configure initial settings.

### 2.1.2 Account Management and Security Settings (Example: Enabling Two-Factor Authentication)

Upon registration, users should regularly review and update personal information to ensure account security. DeepSeek offers multiple security features, including two-factor authentication and password strength detection.

#### Security Recommendations

Change passwords periodically and enable two-factor authentication.

Complete profile details in the account management interface and customize themes and preferences.

## 2.2 User Interface and Functions

DeepSeek's main interface is designed for simplicity and intuitiveness, divided into three key areas:

Text input area: Located at the bottom of the interface for entering instructions or questions.

Output display area: Positioned centrally to showcase AI-generated text or relevant content.

Navigation menu: On the left sidebar, providing access to history, personal settings, and functional entries.

### Example Workflow

When a user opens DeepSeek, they see a clear input box and a large output area. For instance, entering: "Recommend English books suitable for Chinese ninth-grade students" triggers the system to generate a detailed response in the output area while displaying related settings and chat history in the sidebar:

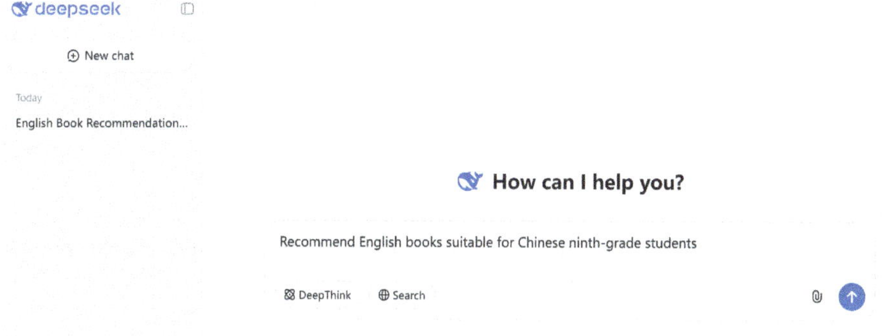

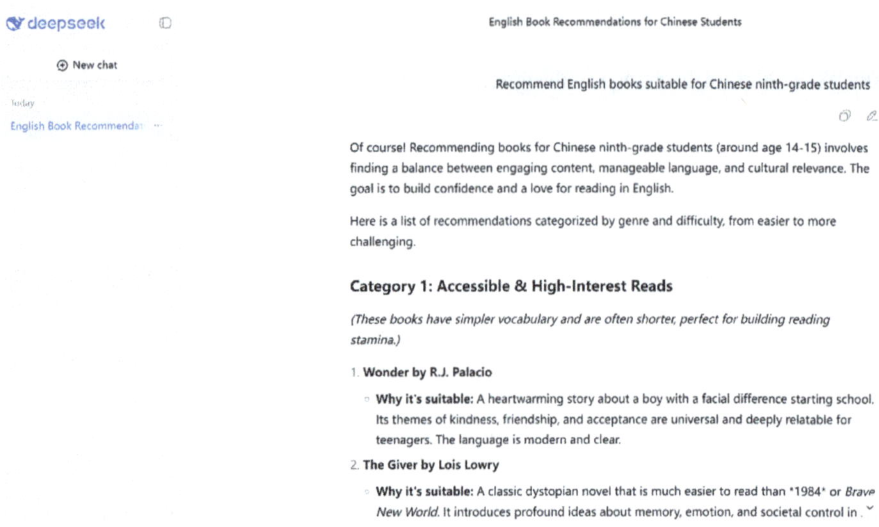


## 2.3 Basic Text Generation and Interactive

### 2.3.1 Text Generation Operations (Example: Auto-Generating Business Reports)

DeepSeek's core strength lies in its advanced text generation capabilities. Users simply describe their needs in detail, and the system rapidly produces compliant text.

#### Example Operation

Input:
"Generate an introduction about the importance of enterprise digital transformation, requiring clear logic, data-backed arguments, and formal expression."

Output:
The system generates a structured introduction covering the background, current status, and future trends of digital transformation.

Refinement:
Users can add follow-up instructions, such as:
"Add a conclusion highlighting strategic implementation detailed steps." The system then adjusts the content accordingly.

### 2.3.2 Feedback and Iterative Optimization (Example: Optimizing Report Content)

In practical use, the initial draft may not fully meet requirements. Users can provide specific revision instructions, enabling DeepSeek to iteratively refine content through multiround feedback.

#### Example Workflow

After generating a draft report, the user identifies insufficient detail in the "Challenges" section and enters:

Add concrete data-backed support to the third paragraph and provide detailed descriptions of the primary challenges.

The system regenerates the revised text, incorporating the requested enhancements.

Users continue interactive feedback for further optimization until satisfaction is achieved.

When using DeepSeek for intelligent content creation and document generation, prompt words play a decisive role. High-quality prompts not only enhance the precision of AI outputs but also significantly improve interaction efficiency. This chapter details the foundational theories, common pitfalls, and optimization methods of prompt engineering. Through ten practical prompt templates and application examples, readers will build a systematic knowledge framework for crafting efficient instructions.

# Chapter 3
# Mastering Prompt Engineering: 10 Strategies for Efficient Interaction

## 3.1 Prompt Engineering Fundamentals

### 3.1.1 Definition and Functions of Prompts (Example: Enhancing Task Accuracy)

Prompts are user instructions guiding the AI to understand task requirements and generate desired outputs. Key functions include:

- Clarifying Needs
  By specifying task details, the AI accurately grasps writing goals.
  Example: Input "Generate a brief report on corporate digital transformation" → the AI focuses on background, current status, and future outlook.
- >Boosting Efficiency
  Detailed prompts reduce redundant information and accelerate target-aligned outputs.
- Reducing Error Rates
  Clear constraints and keywords minimize output deviations (e.g., "Include data-backed evidence").

### 3.1.2 Common Pitfalls and Optimization Tips (Example: Avoiding Ambiguity)

Typical issues when designing prompts:

- Overly Vague Prompts
  Optimization: List explicit requirements (e.g., "Generate a report covering: background, objectives, and data-supported analysis")
- Insufficient Context
  Optimization: Provide background details (e.g., "Include 2024 policy impacts and case studies")
- Unclear Formatting
  Optimization: Specify structures (e.g., "Use bullet points and subheadings")
- Lack of Iterative Feedback
  Optimization: Refine drafts via follow-ups (e.g., "Add statistical details to Section 3")

## 3.2 Ten Prompt Templates and Their Practical Applications

DeepSeek supports diverse prompt templates tailored for different task scenarios.

 | https://doi.org/10.1515/9783112218181-003

### 3.2.1 Task-Oriented Prompts (Example: Report Generation)

Use case: Long-form content (reports, articles).

Template:
"Generate a draft of the '2024 Annual Report on Electronics Industry Development.' Structure: Background, Key Achievements, Challenges, and Future Plans. Use formal language with data-driven insights."

### 3.2.2 Format-Specific Prompts (Example: Tabular Data Output)

Use case: Structured outputs (tables, lists).

Template:
"Present the survey results in a Markdown table with columns: Product Category, 2023–2024 Sales Growth (%), and Market Share Trends."

### 3.2.3 Logic Reasoning Type (Example: Market Data Analysis)

Purpose: Data analysis and causal relationship discussion.

Prompt example: "Analyze the reasons for the decline in sales of new products. List potential factors, their impact levels, and improvement suggestions. Ensure rigorous logic."

### 3.2.4 Creative Generation Type (Example: Short Video Script)

Purpose: Generate ad copy, creative headlines, etc.

Prompt example:
"Generate 5 creative slogans about 'eco-friendly technology,' each ≤10 words. Prioritize originality and ease of dissemination."

### 3.2.5 Data Analysis Type (Example: Market Trend Report)

Purpose: Create research or trend Research Report.

Prompt example:
"Generate a draft Research Report on 'H1 2024 Automotive Market Trends,' including data tables and explanations of key metrics."

### 3.2.6 Code Generation Type (Example: Python Data Analysis Code)

Purpose: Assist programming by generating code snippets.

Prompt example: "Write Python code to calculate the average value of all numbers in a list. Add detailed comments."

### 3.2.7 Multi-round Interaction Type (Example: Iterative Report Optimization)

Purpose: Build complex content step-by-step.

Prompt example:
"Step 1: Generate an outline for a report on 'Corporate Digital Transformation.'
Step 2: Elaborate on the 'Background' section based on the outline.
Step 3: Supplement with practical case studies."

### 3.2.8 Template Completion Type (Example: Official Document Template)

Purpose: Fill in templates or structured reports.

Prompt example:
"Complete the following press release template:
[Title]: . . .
[Body]: . . .
[Conclusion]: . . .
Ensure coherent phrasing."

### 3.2.9 Tone Customization Type (Example: Speech Draft)

Purpose: Draft speeches or texts requiring specific emotional tones.

Prompt example:
"Generate a draft speech on 'Corporate Culture Development.' Use a firm, passionate tone, with each paragraph ≥150 words."

### 3.2.10 Translation and Language Conversion Type (Example: Technical Document Translation)

Purpose: Translate text or convert multilingual content.

Prompt example:
"Translate the following Chinese paragraph into standard American English. Retain professional terminology and formal tone."

## 3.3 Optimization Techniques for Ensuring AI Output Quality

To ensure AI outputs meet expectations, the following optimization strategies are indispensable:

- Step-by-Step Instructions
  Decompose complex tasks into sequential Detailed Steps to guide structured generation.
- Output Style Specification
  Explicitly define format, tone, and structural requirements.
- Output Length Control
  Set precise constraints to prevent verbose or truncated content.
- Iterative Feedback Refinement
  Leverage multi-round interactions for incremental optimization.

# Chapter 4
# DeepSeek in Workplace Efficiency and Business Decision-Making

DeepSeek, as China's leading large-scale AI model, has demonstrated exceptional capabilities across various applications – including email drafting, meeting minutes summarization, work reports, and market research documentation – leveraging its powerful text generation, intelligent Q&A, and data analysis functions. This chapter details how to utilize DeepSeek to assist in drafting and optimizing official documentation, providing concrete operational Detailed Steps and intuitive command examples. These resources enable readers to fully leverage AI capabilities in daily operations and business decision-making, thereby enhancing workplace efficiency.

## 4.1 DeepSeek in Workplace Efficiency and Business Decision-Making

- Functional Overview
  DeepSeek can automatically generate formally structured business emails and correspondence based on user-provided key information, significantly accelerating drafting efficiency.
- Practical Case
  A company needed to send a collaboration intent confirmation email, requiring coverage of: basic information of both parties, collaboration scope, and follow-up plans.
- Operational Detailed Steps
  The user enters the following prompt in the DeepSeek input box:

"Please generate a business email draft regarding 'Confirmation of Cooperation Intent'. The draft should include basic company information, an overview of the cooperation project, cooperation terms, and next-step plans. The tone should be formal and concise."

Please generate a business email draft regarding 'Confirmation of Cooperation Intent'. The draft should include basic company information, an overview of the cooperation project, cooperation terms, and next-step plans. The tone should be formal and concise.

 | https://doi.org/10.1515/9783112218181-004

Please generate a business email draft regarding 'Confirmation of Cooperation Intent'. The draft should include basic company information, an overview of the cooperation project, cooperation terms, and next-step plans. The tone should be formal and concise.

Of course. Here is a formal and concise business email draft for confirming cooperation intent.

**Subject: Confirmation of Cooperation Intent - [Your Company Name] & [Partner Company Name]**

**Dear [Mr./Ms./Mx. Last Name],**

Following our productive discussion on [Date of meeting/call], we are pleased to formally express our intent to proceed with the collaborative project between [Your Company Name] and [Partner Company Name].

**[Your Company Name]**, a leader in [Your Industry] specializing in [Your Company's Specialization], is confident that a partnership with your esteemed organization will be mutually beneficial.

**Project Overview:**
The proposed cooperation, tentatively titled "[Project Name]," aims to [State the primary objective, e.g., "co-develop a new software solution for the logistics sector" or "jointly launch a marketing campaign in the European market"]. We believe that by leveraging [Your Company's] strengths in [Your Key Strength] and [Partner Company's] expertise in [Partner's Key Strength], we can achieve a significant market impact.

**Key Cooperation Terms:**
Based on our initial discussions, we have outlined the following key terms:

The user may add further instructions to refine specific terms after reviewing, such as:

"Please add specific descriptions about the cooperation period and payment terms in the email."

Please add specific descriptions about the cooperation period and payment terms in the email.

DeepThink Search 

After confirming that the email meets basic requirements, the user copies the generated email into office software for fine-tuning and sending:

> Please add specific descriptions about the cooperation period and payment terms in the email.

Of course. Here is the revised email draft with specific descriptions for the cooperation period and payment terms added to the "Key Cooperation Terms" section.

**Subject: Confirmation of Cooperation Intent - [Your Company Name] & [Partner Company Name]**

**Dear [Mr./Ms./Mx. Last Name],**

Following our productive discussion on [Date of meeting/call], we are pleased to formally express our intent to proceed with the collaborative project between [Your Company Name] and [Partner Company Name].

**[Your Company Name]**, a leader in [Your Industry] specializing in [Your Company's Specialization], is confident that a partnership with your esteemed organization will be mutually beneficial.

**Project Overview:**
The proposed cooperation, tentatively titled "[Project Name]," aims to [State the primary objective, e.g., "co-develop a new software solution for the logistics sector" or "jointly launch a marketing campaign in the European market"]. We believe that by leveraging [Your Company's] strengths in [Your Key Strength] and [Partner Company's] expertise in [Partner's Key Strength], we can achieve a significant market impact.

**Key Cooperation Terms:**
Based on our initial discussions, we have outlined the following key terms:

- **Cooperation Period:** The initial term of this agreement is proposed to be **[Number] years**, commencing on [Proposed Start Date, e.g., January 1, 2024]. The agreement will automatically renew for successive one-year periods unless either party provides written notice of non-renewal at least [Number, e.g., 60] days prior to the end of the current term.
- **Payment Terms:**
  - [Partner Company Name] will compensate [Your Company Name] based on a **[Payment Model, e.g., fixed fee of $X / revenue share of Y% / milestone-based payment]** structure.

## 4.2 Intelligent Generation of Meeting Minutes and Work Reports

### 4.2.1 Meeting Minutes

- Functional Overview
  DeepSeek automates the summarization of meeting discussions, extracts key decisions and action plans, and generates structured meeting minutes.
- Case Study
  A company requires rapid generation of minutes for quarterly performance review meetings to facilitate archiving and dissemination.
- Operational Detailed Steps
  Submit meeting audio or transcript to DeepSeek with this prompt: Generate formal meeting minutes based on the following record divided into three sections: Key Discussion Points Decisions Made and Next Actions with critical outcomes emphasized

After receiving the initial draft provide feedback: Add specific responsibilities and deadlines under the Next Actions section.

After iterative adjustments, finalize the meeting minutes for internal distribution and archiving.

### 4.2.2 Work Reports and Project Summaries

- Functional Overview
  DeepSeek efficiently generates work reports and project summaries, systematically consolidating work achievements, identified issues, and improvement strategies.
- Case Study
  The marketing department needs to submit a Q3 2024 work report covering results, key data, and next-phase plans.
- Operational Detailed Steps
  Enter the initial prompt: “Generate a draft ‘Marketing Department Q3 2024 Work Report’ including work achievements, performance data, identified issues, and improvement suggestions. Use bullet points with objective language and logical flow.”

After receiving the system-generated draft, provide feedback: “Add specific sales data tables under Work Achievements and elaborate market challenges in the Issues section.”

Finalize and export the report after iterative adjustments.

## 4.3 Intelligent Generation of Market Research and Research Report

### 4.3.1 Market Research Report

- Functional Overview
  DeepSeek enables automated market research report generation, covering data collection, analysis, and visual chart presentation to support strategic decisions.
- Case Study
  A company requires analysis of H1 2024 automotive market trends, including current market status, competitive landscape, and future projections.
- Operational Detailed Steps
  Input command: "Generate a draft 'H1 2024 Automotive Market Research Report' with sections: Current Market Status, Competitive Analysis, Key Challenges, and Future Trends. Ensure data substantiation and embedded explanatory tables."

Verify data completeness postgeneration and request enhancement: "Add market share and growth rate data for key competitors in Competitive Analysis."

### 4.3.2 Investment Research Report

- Functional Overview
  DeepSeek assists in creating investment Research Report using PEST/SWOT frameworks to evaluate market opportunities/risks and inform investment decisions.
- Case Study
  An investment team needs an emerging industry report detailing market opportunities, potential risks, and actionable recommendations.
- Operational Detailed Steps
  Input command: "Draft an 'Emerging Industry Investment Research Report' covering Market Opportunities, Potential Risks, SWOT Analysis, and Investment Recommendations. Maintain data substantiation and logical rigor."

Refine initial draft via feedback: "Detail SWOT elements (Strengths, Weaknesses, Opportunities, Threats) in tabular format with supporting data."

Save and export report after multiround optimization.

## 4.4 Intelligent Drafting of Resumes, Speeches, and Work Summaries

- Functional Overview
  DeepSeek automatically generates professionally formatted resumes and cover letter templates based on user-provided personal information and professional backgrounds, enhancing their professional image.
- Case Study
  Recent graduate "Xiao Wang" requires a resume containing standard professional components.
- Operational Detailed Steps
  Initiate with command: "Generate a resume draft including personal details, work experience, project highlights, and core skills. Prioritize conciseness with emphasis on key strengths."
  Refine via follow-up: "Optimize the project experience section to highlight specific contributions and quantifiable results."
  Concurrently request cover letter: "Draft a cover letter succinctly stating my competitive advantages and motivation for applying."
  Integrate both documents and save in standardized formats

### 4.4.1 Speeches and Work Summary Reports

- Functional Overview
  DeepSeek produces logically structured speeches and reports with fluent language suitable for public delivery and internal communication.
- Case Study
  Department requiring corporate culture speech draft with accompanying Work Summary Report report.
- Operational Detailed Steps
  Command for speech: "Generate a draft speech on 'Corporate Culture Development' covering three sections: Core Principles (≥150 words), Practical Cases (≥150 words), and Future Outlook (≥150 words)."
  Command for report: "Draft a generic 'Department Work Summary Report Report' outlining primary achievements, existing issues, and improvement suggestions using formal bullet-point formatting."
  Produce finalized versions after iterative refinements.

# Chapter 5
# DeepSeek Applications in Family Education

DeepSeek empowers children to develop self-directed learning, critical thinking, self-drive, research capabilities, reading expansion, academic comprehension, and emotional well-being. By designing precise prompts, clarifying objectives, and leveraging iterative feedback, parents can create an efficient, engaging, and human-centered learning environment. This chapter demonstrates how DeepSeek transcends simple Q&A to actively nurture children's holistic growth when integrated with family education principles.

## 5.1 Cultivating Self-Directed Learning

- Functional Overview
  DeepSeek assists parents in building children's autonomous learning habits through personalized planning, task decomposition, and real-time feedback, transitioning children from passive receivers to active explorers
- Operational Detailed Steps
  (1) Personalized learning plan generation
    - Input the child's academic profile (subjects, weaknesses, available time, etc.) into DeepSeek.

    Prompt example:
    "Generate a personalized learning plan based on: grade level, subject weaknesses, daily available study time . . ."
    After generation, parents can review and request additions/modifications, such as adding weekend review sessions or rest intervals.

  (2) Learning task decomposition and tracking
    Break down complex learning goals (e.g., "complete 3 textbook chapters in 1 week") into specific, executable daily tasks.

    Prompt example:
    "Decompose this week's learning goals into daily tasks with reasonable workload, reserving time for review and preview."
    - After each task, let DeepSeek adjust based on the child's feedback, e.g., shortening single-session duration or adding interest-based activities.

  (3) Interactive self-review and reflection
    - After studying, let the child input problems or insights to DeepSeek.

 | https://doi.org/10.1515/9783112218181-005

Prompt example:
"Generate a reflection report based on the following study records, highlighting key takeaways, difficulties, and improvement suggestions."

Through iterative feedback, help the child understand progress and improvement directions, gradually fostering independent reflection habits.

- Example: Xiao Ming's Weekly Plan
  (1) Initial generation
    - Parent input: "Create a math/English weekly plan for Xiao Ming (7th grade). He has 2 h/weekday and 4 h/weekend."
    - DeepSeek outputs a table with daily tasks, key knowledge points, and review arrangements.

  (2) Feedback and adjustment
    - Parent feedback: "Move Saturday's math review to Sunday morning, and add a 30 min vocabulary quiz on Friday evening."
    - DeepSeek updates and reoutputs the plan automatically.

---

**Optimized Phrase Recommendations**

"Learning plan decomposition," "Reasonable task allocation," "Phased goals," "Daily feedback," "Dynamic adjustments," "Periodic summaries," "Preview-review integration," "Interest guidance," "Adequate rest," "Independent reflection," etc.

---

## 5.2 Critical Thinking Development

- Functional Overview
  Critical thinking encompasses analytical reasoning and multi-perspective analysis. Through multi-round dialogues with DeepSeek, parents can guide children to explore topics multidimensionally.
- Operational Detailed Steps
  (1) Multi-angle inquiry
    - Have children input their views on a topic, and then let DeepSeek provide pro/con arguments.

  Prompt example:
  "Analyze 'online gaming's impact on teens' from both positive and negative angles with supporting evidence."

  (2) Encourage counterquestions
  Guide children to question DeepSeek's answers to foster critical thinking.

Prompt example:
"If someone claims 'online games promote socialization', list possible counterarguments."

(3) Structured summary
   - Let DeepSeek organize discussions into mind maps/key point lists.

   Prompt example:
   "Convert this discussion into a mind map highlighting key branches and conclusions."

- Example: "Online Gaming's Impact on Teens"
  (1) Initial discussion
      Child's input: "Games have pros and cons."
      - DeepSeek lists advantages (relaxation/socialization) and disadvantages (addiction/time waste).
  (2) Counterquestion
      - Child challenges: "Must relaxation rely on games?"
      - DeepSeek offers alternative relaxation methods for comparison.
  (3) Mind map summary
      - Generates a map containing "Pro/Con Arguments" and "Rebuttals."

---

**Optimized Phrase Recommendations**

"Multi-angle analysis, pros and cons arguments, reverse questioning, logical reasoning, mind mapping, structured summarization, questioning spirit, critical thinking, argument sorting, and viewpoint comparison."

---

## 5.3 Self-Drive Cultivation

- Functional Overview
  Fostering children's self-drive requires combining intrinsic interests with external incentives. DeepSeek utilizes gamification or achievement systems to provide positive feedback upon reaching milestones, sustaining learning motivation.
- Operational Detailed Steps
  (1) Interest-driven project design
      Input the child's hobbies and skills to be developed → DeepSeek recommends interdisciplinary projects.

      Prompt example:
      "Design a project combining painting and geography: illustrating continents with key geological features."

(2) Achievement system setup
   - Let DeepSeek design an "Achievement Unlock Mechanism" for children. Unlocking an "Honor Badge" upon completing 5 daily check-ins per week or mastering 20 new vocabulary words.

   Example:
   "Design a 'Learning Achievement System' with tiered badges, unlock conditions, and motivational messages."
(3) Progress-based encouragement
   Parents update progress in DeepSeek to generate automated encouragement or reward plans.

   Example:
   "The child has consistently adhered to a daily 1-hour reading plan for 2 weeks. Generate an encouragement message and propose the next goal."
- Project-Based Learning Example: Integrating Art and Geography
  (1) Preliminary plan
     Parent input: "My child enjoys painting and world maps. Can you design a project-based learning plan to help them understand continental geographic features through drawing?"
     - DeepSeek generated a detailed project idea: for example, choosing one continent each week, researching information, creating illustrative maps, and writing geographical introductions.
  (2) Achievement incentives
     Parent input: "Please set 3 milestones: names of achievement badges and encouraging messages for completing tasks of mapping 2 continents, 4 continents, and all 7 continents."
     - DeepSeek generated badges such as "Explorer" and "Little Globetrotter," along with motivational messages.

---

**Recommended Optimization Phrases**

Interest-driven," "project-based learning," "gamified incentives," "achievement unlocking," "stage-based goals," "self-management," "honor badges," "continuous feedback," "positive reinforcement," "interest integration."

---

## 5.4 Research Skill Development

- Functional Overview
  DeepSeek guides children through the entire research process – topic selection, information retrieval, data analysis, logical reasoning, and report writing – to cultivate investigative thinking and research acumen.
- Operation Detailed Steps
  (1) Topic selection and data collection
  Prompt example:
  "Suggest small research topics on 'climate change impacts on local plants' and list accessible data sources."
  (2) Data analysis and visualization
    - Generates visual charts (e.g., line graphs for temperature trends) and concise analytical conclusions

  Prompt example:
  *Perform statistical analysis on the following data, highlight trends, and generate an executable HTML dashboard: Temperature (°C), Rainfall (mm), Plant Growth: 22,2.5,Good; 24,3,Good; 23,0,Fair; 22,1,Fair.*
  *Output: Generates visual charts (e.g., line graphs for temperature trends) and concise analytical conclusions.*
  (3) Research report drafting
    - Finally, parents can guide their children to ask DeepSeek for help in organizing ideas and drafting the first version of the research report.

Prompt example:
"Draft a research report based on experimental data and conclusions, including Background, Methods, Results, and Discussion sections."
- Example: Small-Scale Climate Study
  (1) Topic selection and data collection
  A child expresses interest in climate change. DeepSeek recommends collecting local temperature, rainfall, and plant germination timing data, along with relevant data sources.
  (2) Data visualization and analysis
    - The child inputs 3 months of observational data into DeepSeek, requesting tables showing monthly average temperature and rainfall trends.
    - DeepSeek generates tables and provides a concise analysis.
  (3) Research report drafting
    - After organizing observations and results, DeepSeek outputs a structured report framework covering Background, Methods, Results, and Conclusions. Parents then guide further refinements, such as adding personal reflections or visuals.

**Optimized Phrase Recommendations**

"research topic selection," "information retrieval," "data visualization," "statistical analysis," "literature citation," "results discussion," "logical inference," "research report drafting," "conclusions and limitations," "future research directions"

## 5.5 Reading Ability Enhancement

- Functional Overview
  Reading volume is an important factor in improving a child's overall abilities. DeepSeek can intelligently recommend appropriate books or articles based on the child's age, interests, and reading level, and assist in generating reading comprehension questions and key summaries to help the child read efficiently.
- Operational Detailed Steps
  (1) Personalized book recommendations
    - Input the child's age, interests, reading goals, etc., and DeepSeek will provide a book list.

  Prompt examples:
  "Based on the interests of a 10-year-old child (historical stories, science fiction, etc.), please recommend 10 suitable Chinese books for them to read, along with a brief introduction for each."
  (2) Reading guidance and Q&A
    - After the child finishes reading part of the material, they can input unclear passages or questions into DeepSeek.

  Prompt example:
  "Please design 5 reading comprehension questions for the following passage and provide brief answers."
  (3) Summary and reflection questions
  To reinforce reading outcomes, DeepSeek can generate a summary or reflection questions for the chapter to help the child deepen understanding.

  Prompt example:
  "Please write a 200-word summary of the following chapter and propose 3 open-ended reflection questions."
- Example: Science Fiction Reading Plan
  (1) Smart book list
  Parent input: "My child is interested in science fiction and wants to read more during the holidays. Could you recommend 5 sci-fi books suitable for a 12-year-old?"
  DeepSeek outputs book titles, authors, difficulty levels, summaries, etc.

(2) Reading comprehension and reflection
When the child is halfway through reading, the parent inputs: "Please design 5 reading comprehension questions for this passage and provide correct answers."

DeepSeek automatically generates questions and answers to help the child check their understanding.

(3) Summary and extension
Parent input: "Please provide a summary of the main plot of this book and propose 2 reflection questions to help the child think further about the story's background."

DeepSeek outputs a summary and open-ended questions to guide deeper thinking.

---

**Optimized Phrase Recommendations**

"Smart Book List Recommendations, Interest Categories, Reading Comprehension Questions, Summary Generation, Reflection Questions, Knowledge Expansion, Paragraph Analysis, Plot Summary, Reading Feedback, Multi-round Interaction"

---

## 5.6 Using DeepSeek to Effectively Tutor Children's Schoolwork

– Functional Overview
In addition to improving overall competence, parents are also very concerned about their children's academic performance in specific subjects. DeepSeek can act as a "personalized tutor," providing professional guidance at home, from problem-solving strategies and error analysis to homework review.

– Operation Detailed Steps

(1) Difficult problem explanation and guidance
When children encounter difficult problems, they can directly input photos or descriptions of the questions into DeepSeek.

Prompt example:
"Please explain in detail the solution strategy for this quadratic function application problem and provide step-by-step calculations."

(2) Error collection and reflection
Parents can compile their children's incorrect answers and ask DeepSeek to analyze the reasons for the mistakes and provide correction strategies.

Prompt example:
"Here are my child's recent math mistakes. Please analyze the error types and suggest targeted practice exercises."

(3) Learning progress tracking and feedback
Parents can regularly input their child's homework completion status into DeepSeek to generate progress reports, highlighting improvements and weaknesses.

Prompt example:
"This week my child completed 20 application problems and made 5 mistakes. Please generate a progress report and suggest exercises for next week."

(4) Example: Math problem tutoring
Initial explanation:
The child inputs a comprehensive quadratic function problem into DeepSeek, which outputs detailed solution, Detailed Steps, and key points to note.
Error collection and improvement:
After repeated mistakes on similar problems, parents input the records into DeepSeek to generate a targeted practice plan.
Progress feedback:
DeepSeek generates a report pointing out weaknesses in formula memorization and solution details, along with targeted practice suggestions.

---

**Optimized Phrase Recommendations**

"Problem-Solving Analysis," "Thinking Guidance," "Error Analysis," "Error Types," "Targeted Practice," "Progress Tracking," "Homework Grading," "Process Explanation," "Personalized Tutoring," "Continuous Improvement"

---

## 5.7 Provide Emotional Support and Psychological Education Using DeepSeek

- Functional Overview
  Beyond academic learning, children also require emotional support and psychological counseling. While DeepSeek cannot replace professional psychologists, it assists parents in understanding children's mental states through emotion analysis and confiding advice, enabling timely care and intervention.
- Operational Detailed Steps
  (1) Emotion recognition and counseling advice
  Parents input the child's daily emotions or stress sources for tailored coping strategies.

  Prompt example:
  "My child has been feeling down lately and lacks motivation for studying. Please provide comforting words and psychological counseling suggestions based on this description."

(2) Learning pressure monitoring and adjustment
Generate self-assessment questionnaires to evaluate stress levels and offer relief techniques.

Prompt example:
"Create a stress self-test questionnaire suitable for middle school students, including simple stress-relief tips."

(3) Parent-child communication and emotional education
Recommend interactive activities to strengthen family bonds.

Prompt example:
"Suggest 5 parent-child interactive games for weekends at home to enhance communication and emotional connection."

Example: Child Emotion Management

(1) Child emotion management
Preliminary counseling

Input: Child's recent behavior (e.g., low motivation).

Output: Encouraging messages + stress-relief techniques (e.g., deep breathing, exercise)

(2) Stress self-assessment questionnaire
DeepSeek generates a 10-question test based on age and academic intensity, providing targeted coping strategies.

(3) Parent-child interaction
Recommends games like Role-Playing Theater or DIY Crafts to ease tension and foster a positive family atmosphere

**Optimized Phrase Recommendations**

Emotion Recognition | Counseling Advice | Psychological Support | Stress Self-Assessment | Emotional Care | Parent-Child Communication | Affective Education | Interactive Games | Positive Reinforcement | Atmosphere Building

## 5.8 Time Management Optimization

- Functional Overview
  Time management is critical for Chinese parents amid heavy academic workloads. DeepSeek creates personalized schedules, tracks execution, and provides feedback to prevent inefficiency or procrastination.

- Operational Detailed Steps
  (1) Schedule planning and prioritization
  Parents input daily tasks (e.g., homework, extracurriculars, and rest periods).

  Prompt example:
  *"Generate a time management table with priorities and reminders for 2 h of study and 1.5 h of evening revision."*
  - DeepSeek outputs a table with segmented time allocations and priorities, making it easy for the child to understand intuitively.

  (2) Daily progress tracking and feedback
  - Children report task completion status daily.

  Prompt example:
  "Analyze my child's task completion efficiency on Monday and suggest improvements."
  - Output: Identifies delays (e.g., "postdinner procrastination") and proposes optimizations like adjusting leisure duration.

  (3) Long-term pattern optimization
  - Parents can summarize their child's time usage weekly or monthly to identify patterns and make adjustments.

  Prompt example:
  "Based on the child's execution records over the past two weeks, please generate a time usage Research Report and suggest adjustments for the next phase."
- Example: Xiaolin's Time Management Plan
  (1) Initial planning
  Parent input:
  "Xiaolin spends 2 h on homework after school, 1.5 h on review and reading after dinner, attends interest classes on Saturday mornings, and engages in outdoor activities on Sunday afternoons. Please generate a detailed schedule."

  DeepSeek output:
  Generates a segmented timetable with activity-intensity labels:
  (2) Feedback and refinement
  "On Wednesday, revision was delayed until 22:00 after dinner."
  DeepSeek analysis:
  Excessive leisure time postdinner (45 min → 110 min)
  Task-initiation resistance ("starting friction")

**Optimized Phrase Recommendations**

"Time Segmentation," "Task Prioritization," "Procrastination Analysis," "Progress Tracking," "Long-term Planning," "Dynamic Adjustment," "Efficient Fragmented Time Utilization," "Timely Review," "Periodic Evaluation," "Self-Monitoring"

## 5.9 Using DeepSeek to Enhance Children's Holistic Learning Abilities

- Functional Overview
  Academic improvement encompasses not only test scores or subject-specific performance but also learning methodologies, knowledge transfer, and comprehensive application skills. DeepSeek provides systematic learning enhancement strategies for children through three core approaches: methodological guidance, resource recommendations, and learning assessment.
- Operational Detailed Steps
  (1) Learning bottleneck diagnosis
    - Parents collect the child's academic data, including:

    Exam scores, daily homework performance, and self-evaluation feedback. Input data into DeepSeek for analysis.

    Prompt example:
    "Based on the following academic records and the child's feedback, identify key learning bottlenecks and propose targeted improvement strategies."

  (2) Resource recommendations and method guidance
    DeepSeek recommends suitable learning materials and methods for different subjects and types of learning bottlenecks.

    Prompt example:
    "Recommend efficient memorization techniques and practice resources for an upper-elementary student struggling with text recitation, addressing his specific weaknesses."

  (3) Comprehensive assessment and iteration
    - Regularly input the child's progress data into DeepSeek, and the system will output a comprehensive assessment report with actionable next-step recommendations.

    Prompt example:
    "Generate a learning capability assessment report evaluating progress in comprehension, memory, and application, then propose future improvement directions."

- Example: Chinese Comprehension and Application Enhancement
  (1) Initial diagnosis
  Parent inputs: Recent Chinese exam scores, essay feedback, and the child's complaint: "I can't memorize texts."

  DeepSeek's analysis:
  Low memorization efficiency and superficial comprehension.

  Solutions: Mind mapping, text-image association exercises.
  (2) Continuous improvement
  - One month later: Parent inputs progress data after using mind mapping.
  DeepSeek generates an assessment report highlighting.

---

**Optimized Phrase Recommendations**

"Learning bottleneck diagnosis," "efficient memorization," "mind mapping," "knowledge transfer," "application skills," "resource recommendation," "continuous improvement," "comprehensive assessment," "staged learning," "dynamic adjustment"

---

## 5.10 Applications of DeepSeek in Family Education

- Functional Overview
  Stable and excellent academic performance is often underpinned by good habits. DeepSeek not only assists children in formulating habit-cultivation plans but also helps identify factors that "undermine good habits" through iterative feedback, enabling timely correction.
- Operation Detailed Steps
  (1) Operational detailed steps
  Parents and children jointly define target habits (e.g., "memorize vocabulary for 10 min daily," "organize desk before bed") and input them into DeepSeek.

  Prompt example:
  "Create a habit checklist including daily vocabulary review, knowledge recap, and desk organization, with specific implementation Detailed Steps."
  (2) Monitoring and feedback
  - Children record daily/weekly progress → DeepSeek generates efficiency reports and analysis.

  Prompt example:
  "Analyze reasons for low completion rates in this week's habit records and suggest improvements."

(3) Positive reinforcement and periodic review
DeepSeek designs milestone rewards or encouragement to sustain motivation.

Prompt example:
"Draft encouraging words praising the child for 14 consecutive days of morning vocabulary practice, and propose the next micro-goal."

- Example: Morning Vocabulary and Desk Organization
  (1) Initial checklist
  Parent input: "Design a schedule for daily morning vocabulary (10 mins) and bedtime desk organization."
    - DeepSeek outputs a table with timelines, methods, and precautions.

  (2) Tracking and adjustment
  After 1 week:
    - Vocabulary practice maintained, but desk organization occasionally missed.
    - DeepSeek diagnosis: "Insufficient bedtime time management" → Suggests "prepone routines by 5 mins for dedicated tidying."

---

**Optimized Phrase Recommendations**

"Habit Checklist," "Positive Reinforcement," "Phase Retrospective," "Completion Rate Tracking," "Habit-Undermining Factors," "Self-Monitoring," "Long-Term Consistency," "Short-Term Targets," "Behavior Tracking," "Immediate Feedback"

---

## 5.11 Facilitating Family Education with DeepSeek

- Functional Overview
  In China's educational context, parent-school collaboration is crucial. DeepSeek enables parents to communicate effectively with teachers and track children's school performance for timely adjustments.
- Operational Detailed Steps
  (1) Communication drafting and strategy
  Parents can use DeepSeek to generate concise emails or inquiries based on their child's academic status.

  Prompt example:
  "Help me draft a brief email to the homeroom teacher describing my child's recent learning state and key questions."

(2) Parent-teacher conference reports
   - For conferences, DeepSeek assists in creating home-performance summaries.

   Prompt example:
   "Generate a parent-teacher conference report covering recent home-learning progress, challenges, and targeted suggestions."
(3) Continuous tracking and feedback
   Input teacher feedback into DeepSeek to generate actionable plans.

   Prompt example:
   "The teacher noted my child's lack of focus in class. Provide family strategies, including schedules and attention-training methods."

- Example: Email Communication with Teacher
  (1) Initial email
     Parent input: "My child struggles with focus during home study. Draft a polite email to inquire about classroom behavior."
     - DeepSeek outputs a courteous email draft.
  (2) Follow-up plan
     - After teacher feedback, parent input: "Based on the teacher's input, create an improvement plan focusing on home routines and environment."
     - DeepSeek generates a targeted Family Education strategy.

---

**Optimized Phrase Recommendations**

"Home-school communication," "polite emails," "brief reports," "targeted suggestions," "class teacher feedback," "family cooperation strategies," "scheduling arrangements," "attention training," "follow-up," and "feedback loop."

---

## 5.12 Use DeepSeek to Enhance Children's Overall Competence

- Functional Overview
  In addition to academic knowledge and mental health, Chinese parents also hope their children will develop in a well-rounded way in areas such as arts, sports, and social practice. DeepSeek can integrate children's interests and goals to provide diversified competence development programs.
- Operational Detailed Steps
  (1) Interest and resource mining
     - Enter the child's strengths, hobbies, and available time.

Prompt example:
"Suggest weekend home-based enrichment projects combining music and handicrafts."

(2) Activity planning & goal setting
Define project objectives, timelines, and material lists.

Prompt example:
"Design a music + handicraft activity plan to enhance artistic appreciation and hands-on skills

(3) Summary and sharing
- Input the child's experience → DeepSeek generates showcase materials (speeches/PPT outlines).

Prompt example:
"Generate a class presentation script based on this activity."

Example: Music and Handicraft Integration Project

(1) Preliminary planning
Parent input: "My child is interested in both music and painting. Please design a small weekend project that allows them to both perform a piece of music and create a handicraft related to the theme of the piece."
DeepSeek output: A comprehensive plan for "making a simple instrument + themed poster," with a list of required materials.

(2) Presentation of result
After completion, the parent submits details of the child's experience, and DeepSeek generates a speech draft or PowerPoint outline to help the child share their project in class.

---

**Optimized Phrase Recommendations**

"Interest integration," "artistic aesthetics," "hands-on ability," "comprehensive practice," "activity planning," "goal setting," "presentation of results," "diversified development," "speech draft," "creative expression"

---

# Chapter 6
# Applications of DeepSeek in Daily

This chapter uses DeepSeek as a tool to systematically present 15 application cases of daily writing projects, covering multiple areas such as social media copywriting, travel, home renovation, health, finance, and parent-child activities. Each case is divided into three Detailed Steps: text input, partial feedback, and multi-round iteration. Through detailed operational instructions and professional optimization phrase recommendations, it achieves precise text generation and personalized adjustments, helping users improve their quality of life and decision-making efficiency.

## 6.1 Social Media Copy Generation

- Functional Overview
  Utilizing DeepSeek to auto-generate creative social posts (e.g., WeChat Moments copy), helping users publish aesthetically engaging, emotionally resonant content that reflects personal style and lifestyle taste.
- Operational Workflow
  (1) Text input and initial draft
  Enter requirements in DeepSeek dialog box, e.g.:
  "Generate a WeChat Moments post describing the joy of weekend city walks. Use vivid language and sincere emotions."
  Output: System returns a draft with scene depictions and emotional expressions.
  (2) Feedback and targeted revision
  Review draft and provide granular feedback, e.g.:
  "Optimize the middle paragraph by adding sensory details, e.g., 'the warmth of street-corner coffee aroma.'"
  Output: Revised copy with enhanced imagery and emotional impact.
  (3) Multi-round iteration to finalization
  Repeat feedback cycles until achieving stylistic consistency, fluency, and precision.

**Optimized Phrase Recommendations**

"Brilliant prose," "sincere emotions," "beautiful language," "vivid imagery," "tight structure," "precise expression," "rich rhetoric," "harmonious rhythm," "warm atmosphere," "unique style," etc.

 | https://doi.org/10.1515/9783112218181-006

## 6.2 Ceremonial Speech Writing

- Functional Overview
  Automating formal speeches (e.g., toasts, wedding congratulations, and birthday wishes) for banquets, gatherings, and festivals, ensuring culturally appropriate and heartfelt delivery.
- Operational Workflow
  (1) Text input and initial draft
  Specify occasion and theme in DeepSeek, e.g.: "Write a company annual gala toast celebrating team success. Include congratulatory messages, team motivation, and positive energy."
  Output: Draft with core congratulations and motivational content.
  (2) Feedback and targeted revision
  Refine based on review, e.g.:
  "Add a captivating opening hook and emphasize team collaboration in the middle section."
  Output: Revised speech with intensified emotion and clearer structure.
  (3) Multi-round iteration to finalization
  Iterate until the speech fully aligns with contextual requirements.

---

**Optimized Phrase Recommendations**

"Impressive," "appropriate language," "passionate," "inspiring," "tight structure," "captivating opening," "clear layers," "emotional," "sincere blessings," "beautiful rhetoric," etc.

---

## 6.3 AI-Powered Travel Planning

- Functional Overview
  Automatically generates personalized travel itineraries based on user inputs (destination, duration, budget, interests), providing day-by-day schedules, attraction details, transportation routes, and dining recommendations to ensure seamless travel experiences.
- Operation Detailed Steps
  (1) Text input and initial draft
  Enter requirements in DeepSeek dialog, e.g.:
  "Generate a 5-day Singapore itinerary including daily activities, attraction introductions, transit options, and food recommendations."
  Output: The system returns a preliminary itinerary with detailed listings of daily activity schedules and attraction recommendations.

(2) Feedback and targeted revision
Review draft and provide granular feedback, e.g.:
"Add zoo visit details on Day 3 with specific MRT line instructions from City Hall Station."
Output: Revised itinerary with enhanced logistics and contextual tips.

(3) Multi-round iteration to finalization
Repeat cycles until achieving route rationality, transport clarity, and experience optimization.

---

**Optimized Phrase Recommendations**

"Reasonable itinerary, rich attractions, convenient transportation, recommended dining, attention to detail, comprehensive information, practicality, thorough planning, accurate recommendations, and optimized experience."

---

## 6.4 Home Renovation Strategy

- Functional Overview
  Creates customized renovation plans for aging properties, comparing design styles, budget tiers, and material options while outlining phased workflows and risk mitigation measures.
- Operational Workflow
  (1) Text input and initial draft
  Input renovation requirements (e.g., "Old house renovation plan") with the command:
  "Generate a comprehensive renovation strategy comparing design styles and budget options, with detailed workflows and critical precautions."
  Output: Draft plan with style comparisons (e.g., Modern Minimalist vs. Rustic Industrial) and cost breakdowns (c.g., matcrial/labor ratios).
  (2) Feedback and refinement
  Provide feedback:
  "Elaborate on material cost details (unit price/quantity/supplier recommendations) and refine workflow descriptions with phase-specific timelines."
  Output: Enhanced plan with: material cost tables, phased workflows.
  (3) Multi-round iteration
  Iterate until achieving an actionable and exhaustive guide.

**Optimized Phrase Recommendations**

"Reasonable plan," "detailed costs," "clear process," "stylish design," "rich in detail," "accurate budget," "detailed materials," "standardized Detailed Steps," "overall coordination," "practical and efficient" . . .

## 6.5 Home Organization Plan Generation

- Function Overview
  Leverage DeepSeek to automatically generate home organization plans, optimizing space utilization for enhanced tidiness and comfort.
- Operation Detailed Steps
  (1) Text input and initial output
  Input requirements (e.g., "Living room & bedroom organization") with the command:
  "Generate a home organization plan for the living room and bedroom, detailing storage methods and tidying techniques."
  (2) Feedback and refinement
  Provide feedback:
  "Add detailed wardrobe organization strategies for the bedroom and refine item categorization for the living room."
  Output: Enhanced plan with well-thought-out details (e.g., wardrobe compartment division) and practical methods for item categorization.
  (3) Multi-round iteration
  Iterate until finalizing a comprehensive and actionable plan with efficient use of space.

**Optimized Phrase Recommendations**

"Clever storage," "reasonable design," "well-thought-out details," "clear categorization," "clear structure," "practical methods," "easy to use," "efficient use of space," "unique creativity," "significant results"

## 6.6 Health-Focused Weight Management

- Function Overview
  Automatically generate health-focused weight management plans with DeepSeek, designing scientifically tailored dietary regimens and workout routines to achieve sustainable weight loss goals.

- Operation Detailed Steps
  (1) Text input and initial output
  Input health metrics (e.g., "Current weight 85 kg, target 65 kg") with the command:
  "Generate a 3-month weight loss plan including daily meals, exercise schedules, and phased milestones."
  (2) Feedback and refinement
  Provide feedback:
  "Elaborate on strength training and cardio protocols with execution details, and optimize macronutrient distribution in the diet."
  (3) Multi-round iteration
  Iterate until finalizing a comprehensive and actionable plan with measurable weekly targets and adaptive adjustments.

---

**Optimized Phrase Recommendations**

"Nutritionally balanced," "calorie control," "exercise planning," "carefully selected ingredients," "scientifically balanced," "easy to follow," "flexible adjustments," "data-driven," "clear goals," and "significant results."

---

## 6.7 Family Savings and Financial Planning

- Function Overview
  Leverage DeepSeek to formulate family savings and financial plans, enabling rational income allocation and expenditure management for steady wealth growth.
- Operation Detailed Steps
  (1) Text input and initial output
  Input financial data (e.g., "Monthly income ¥10k, expenditure ¥6k") with the command:
  "Generate a 1-year family financial plan including income allocation, savings strategy, and investment recommendations."
  (2) Feedback and refinement
  Provide feedback:
  "Elaborate on investment strategies with risk control measures and emergency reserve suggestions."
  (3) Multi-round iteration
  *Iterate until finalizing a structurally complete and actionable plan with robust data support.

**Optimized Phrase Recommendations**

"Clear budget," "risk control," "scientific investment," "financial stability," "detailed planning," "reasonable allocation," "data support," "clear strategy," "easy operation," and "significant benefits."

## 6.8 Invitation Generator

- Function Overview
  Automate event invitations with DeepSeek to craft formal yet warm messages, ensuring precise information delivery.
- Operation Detailed Steps
  (1) Text input and initial output
  Input request (e.g., "Family gathering invitation") with the command:
  "Generate a family gathering invitation including event time, venue, activities, and precautions."
  Output: Draft invitation with formal structure and detailed content.
  (2) Feedback and refinement
  Provide feedback:
  "Add specific activity arrangements and refine the language for a more approachable tone."
  Output: Optimized invitation with warmer tone and clearer information.
  (3) Multi-round iteration
  Iterate until achieving a perfect balance of formality and approachability.

**Optimized Phrase Recommendations**

"Formal format," "detailed content," "friendly language," "clear structure," "complete information," "well-organized," "concise wording," "accurate expression," "unique creativity," "appropriate etiquette," etc.

## 6.9 Shopping Comparison and Product

- Function Overview
  Use DeepSeek to automatically generate shopping comparison reports and product review guides, helping users compare product performance, prices, and user reviews to make rational purchasing decisions.

- Operation Detailed Steps
  (1) Text input and initial output
  Input product details (e.g., “Smartphones”) with the command:
  “Generate a smartphone comparison report covering performance, pricing, user reviews, and after-sales service.”
  Output: Initial report with comparison tables and evaluation insights.
  (2) Feedback and refinement
  Provide feedback:
  “Add concrete user review examples and elaborate on after-sales policies.”
  Output: Enhanced report with case studies and precise data.
  (3) Multi-round iteration
  Iterate until achieving a thorough, data-driven review guide.

---

**Optimized Phrase Recommendations**

“Detailed comparison, comprehensive evaluation, accurate data, objective analysis, practical recommendations, clear structure, rich content, rigorous logic, case studies, and smart shopping.” . . . . . .

---

## 6.10 Family Parent-Child Activity Planning

- Function Overview
  Leverage DeepSeek to automatically generate family activity plans, designing diverse and engaging activities that enhance parent-child bonding and strengthen family cohesion.
- Operation Detailed Steps
  (1) Text input and initial output
  Input requirements (e.g., “Weekend outdoor activities and DIY crafts”) with the command:
  “Generate a family activity plan including outdoor exploration, DIY crafts, and interactive games.”
  (2) Feedback and refinement
  Provide feedback:
  “Add safety precautions and rest intervals for outdoor activities, and specify required materials for DIY crafts.”
  Output: Enhanced plan with improved practicality and safety measures.
  (3) Multi-round iteration
  Iterate until finalizing a detailed, creatively rich activity plan.

**Optimized Phrase Recommendations**

"Rich activities," "strong interactivity," "safety and security," "reasonable arrangements," "attention to detail," "creativity," "parent-child integration," "time optimization," "fun," "easy to implement," etc.

## 6.11 Life Hacks and DIY Solutions Generator

- Function Overview
  Automate family activity planning with DeepSeek to design diverse parent-child interactions, strengthening family bonding.
- Operation Detailed Steps
  (1) Text input and initial output
  Input DIY requests (e.g., "Home Storage DIY Solution") into DeepSeek, with the command:
  "Generate a detailed DIY home storage guide including operational Detailed Steps, required materials, and precautions."
  Output: The system generates an initial guide listing specific Operation Detailed Steps and material list.
  (2) Feedback and refinement
  Provide feedback:
  "Add safety precautions and rest intervals to outdoor activities, and specify required materials for DIY crafts." Output: Enhanced plan with operational safety and material details.
  (3) Multi-round iteration
  Iterate until achieving a creative, safety-optimized activity plan.

**Optimized Phrase Recommendations**

"Easy to use," "clear Detailed Steps," "complete materials," "detailed instructions," "illustrated with text and images," "endless creativity," "practical and efficient," "specific prompts," "easy to execute," "significant results"

## 6.12 Developing a Healthy Eating Plan

- Function Overview
  Automatically generate healthy diet recipes with DeepSeek to design scientifically balanced daily meal plans that meet nutritional requirements.

- Operation Detailed Steps
  (1) Text input and initial output
  → Input dietary needs (e.g., "Low-calorie healthy eating") with the command: "Generate a 1-week low-calorie healthy diet plan including three daily meal suggestions and nutritional pairing."
  Output: Initial recipe listing meal suggestions and calorie details.
  (2) Feedback and refinement
  → Provide feedback:
  "Add high-protein, low-fat ingredient options for dinner and specify cooking methods."
  (3) Multi-round iteration
  Iterate until achieving a comprehensive, science-based meal plan.

**Optimized Phrase Recommendations**

"Nutritionally balanced," "calorie control," "fresh ingredients," "healthy cooking," "scientific plan," "easy to follow," "flexible adjustments," "excellent taste," "accurate data," "significant results," etc.

## 6.13 Develop a Kitchen Cleaning Strategy

- Function Overview
  Leverage DeepSeek to automatically generate kitchen-cleaning guides, designing efficient cleaning workflows and practical techniques that tackle daily grease buildup and clutter issues.
- Operation Detailed Steps
  (1) Text input and initial output
  → Input request (e.g., "Kitchen grease cleaning") with the command:
  "Generate a kitchen degreasing guide including step-by-step instructions, required cleaning agents, and precautions."
  (2) Feedback and refinement
  Provide feedback:
  "Add instructions for handling stubborn stains and optimize the sequence of Detailed Steps."
  Output: Enhanced guide with clearer sequencing and stain-specific techniques.
  (3) Multi-round iteration
  Iterate until achieving a practical, household-adapted cleaning strategy.

**Optimized Phrase Recommendations**

"Simple to operate, clear Detailed Steps, innovative methods, significant results, thorough cleaning, complete details, easy to understand, practical and efficient, rich in techniques, problem solving."

## 6.14 Running Training Plan

- Function Overview
  Automate fitness planning with DeepSeek to design running regimens that boost endurance and health metrics.
- Operation Detailed Steps
  (1) Text input and initial output
  → Input goal (e.g., "Build endurance from daily jogging") with the command: "Generate a 3-month running plan specifying daily duration, intensity levels, and rest schedules."
  Output: Initial plan covering running distances and timelines.
  (2) Feedback and refinement
  → Provide feedback:
  "Integrate strength training and stretching routines, with phase-specific objectives."
  Output: Comprehensive plan with cross-training and milestone targets.
  (3) Multi-round iteration
  Iterate until finalizing an actionable, scientifically optimized training program.

**Optimized Phrase Recommendations**

"Detailed plan, clear objectives, distinct stages, scientific training, reasonable timing, standardized movements, adequate rest, significant results, data-driven, and easy to operate."

# Chapter 7
# Applications of DeepSeek in Content Innovation and Intelligent Writing for Social Media

DeepSeek, as a leading domestic large language model, possesses not only powerful text generation capabilities but can also perform diversified style customization, structural optimization, and multimodal information integration based on user needs. This chapter systematically introduces how to utilize DeepSeek for intelligent creation of self-media content, covering the process from creative conception and text generation, style customization to multimodal content generation and integration, and extending to video scriptwriting, interactive copy creation, and search engine optimization (SEO) article writing. Through specific operation Detailed Steps and intuitive prompt examples, readers can comprehensively master practical methods for AI-assisted content creation, thereby excelling in self-media operations and achieving efficient output and precise dissemination.

## 7.1 Creative Ideation and Content Planning (Example: Generating a Content)

- Function Overview
  Self-media creation first requires creative conception and content planning. DeepSeek can quickly generate creative outlines and conceptual plans based on user-input themes, keywords, and target audiences, providing an initial framework for content creation.
- Operation Detailed Steps and Prompt Examples
  (1) Determine theme and keywords
  * Example: Theme "Environmental Technology," keywords include "Sustainable Development," "Green Energy," etc.
  (2) Generate creative outline
  Prompt example: "Please generate a content creation outline on 'Environmental Technology', requiring inclusion of theme background, core viewpoints, creative expression, and expected outcomes. Language should be concise and clear."
  (3) Initial feedback and adjustment
  * Based on the generated results, users can append instructions like: "Please add specific examples of 'green energy applications' to the core viewpoints section."

 | https://doi.org/10.1515/9783112218181-007

## 7.2 DeepSeek's Application in Self-Media Content Innovation and Intelligent Writing

- Function Overview
  DeepSeek possesses high-quality text generation capabilities, able to generate articles in various genres according to specified style requirements, including press releases, commentaries, essays, and poetry.
- Operation Detailed Steps and Prompt Example
  (1) Generate creative paragraphs
  Example: "Please generate a paragraph describing 'Future Cities' for a short video script. Require language full of futurism and technological sense, each sentence no more than 15 words, using vivid metaphors."
  (2) Style customization
  Users can further specify the genre: "Please generate a modern poem about 'Digital Life', requiring fresh language, rich rhythm, with each stanza having at least 4 lines."
  (3) Multi-round feedback
  If parts of the initial draft do not meet requirements, append instructions like: "Please adjust the second stanza to a more relaxed and humorous style, adding specific scene descriptions."

## 7.3 Creative Ideation and Content Planning (Example: Generating a Content Creation Outline)

- Function Overview
  In self-media creation, combining text and images has become mainstream. DeepSeek can interface with image generation tools, generating theme-compliant images through detailed text descriptions, or assisting in creating infographics, enhancing the content's visual appeal.
- Operation Detailed Steps and Prompt Example
  (1) Generate image descriptions
  Example: "Please generate 5 detailed image descriptions about 'Future City Nightscapes'. Each description must include main buildings, lighting effects, and color schemes, using vivid language."
  (2) Interface with image generation tools
  Users copy the generated descriptions to an image generation platform (e.g., "Jimeng AI") for batch generation, followed by fine-tuning the images.
  (3) Integrate text and image content
  Prompt example: "Please generate a self-media article integrating the above image descriptions and textual explanations. Require a clear content structure, incorporating tables and images for visual presentation."

## 7.4 Video Script and Interactive Copywriting (Example: Writing Scripts for Short Videos)

- Function Overview
  Short videos and live streaming have become important forms of dissemination in self-media. DeepSeek can assist in generating video scripts, hosting scripts, and interactive copy, helping creators quickly conceive and output high-quality video content.
- Operation Detailed Steps and Prompt Example
  (1) Writing a video script outline
  Prompt example: "Please generate a short video script outline about 'Environmental Technology', including an opening, main content presentation, and a closing call to action. The language should be friendly and engaging."
  (2) Generating the full script
  Based on the outline, the user can add the instruction: "Please write detailed content for each part of the outline, especially emphasizing interactive segments and audience questions."
  (3) Generating interactive copy
  Prompt example: "Please generate 3 interactive question copies about 'Environmental Technology'. The language should be light, fun, and capable of encouraging audience participation."

## 7.5 SEO Article and Advertising Copy Optimization (Example: Precise Keyword Optimization)

- Function Overview
  In self-media operations, the quality of SEO and advertising copy directly impacts content dissemination effectiveness. DeepSeek can optimize text content based on keywords, making drafts more attractive and shareable.
- Operation Detailed Steps and Prompt Example
  (1) Generating an SEO article draft
  Prompt example: "Please generate an SEO article draft about 'The Future of Green Energy', including a title, body, and conclusion. Ensure the keywords 'green energy' and 'sustainable development' are evenly distributed, and the language is easy to understand."
  (2) Advertising copy generation
  Prompt example: "Please generate 5 advertising copy lines about 'Eco-friendly Products', each no longer than 12 characters. The content should be vivid, concise, and attractive.""
  (3) Feedback and refinement
  Based on the draft's effectiveness, the user may add the instruction: "Please enhance the advertising copy by adding emotional words and a call to action."

# Chapter 8
# DeepSeek in Finance and Investment Decision-Making

In financial markets, where data complexity and variables abound, investment decisions rely on precise data analysis and scientific model forecasting. Leveraging advanced natural language processing (NLP) and large-scale data processing capabilities, DeepSeek rapidly extracts high-value insights from massive information and generates detailed analytical reports. This chapter details DeepSeek's applications across five financial scenarios: individual stock analysis, industry sector research, industry risk assessment, market trend forecasting, and quantitative trading strategy development. Each section includes operation Detailed Steps and practical command examples.

(Editor's note: This chapter provides an overview of the functions of AI in finance-related fields and does not involve specific investment advice.)

## 8.1 Individual Stock Analysis and Investment Recommendations (Example: Financial Analysis of Listed Companies)

- Core Function
  Integrates financial reports, news, and market data to comprehensively analyze a target company's fundamentals, financial status, and competitive advantages, generating actionable investment recommendations.
- Operation Detailed Steps
  (1) Data preparation
  Collect the target company's stock code, key financial metrics (revenue, net profit, debt-to-asset ratio), and recent news.
  (2) Initial draft generation
  Command example:
  "Generate a draft Research Report for stock 'SZ000XXX', covering company fundamentals, key financial indicators, market competitiveness, and risk alerts. Use formal language and data-rich content."
  (3) Feedback and refinement
  If you find that the financial data is insufficient, you can add the following instruction: "Please add the year-on-year growth rate and profit margin trends for the past three years to the financial analysis section and generate relevant data charts."
  (4) Finalize output
  Generate a standardized industry report for strategic planning.

 | https://doi.org/10.1515/9783112218181-008

## 8.2 Industry Sector Analysis (Example: Analysis of the New Energy Vehicle Industry)

- Core Function
  Integrates macroeconomic data, competitive landscapes, and policy environments to generate comprehensive industry reports, identifying market opportunities and risks.
- Operation Detailed Steps
  (1) Data collection
  Compile market data, competitor information, and policy updates for target industries (e.g., new energy vehicles and internet finance).
  (2) Generate a draft
  Prompt example: "Please generate a draft Research Report on the 'new energy vehicle' industry sector, including market status, competitive landscape, and policy environment. The text should be objective, the data comprehensive, and charts should be included for clarification."
  (3) Feedback and adjustments
  Additional instructions: "Please provide a detailed description of the impacts of supply chain disruptions and policy changes in the risk assessment section, and conduct a detailed comparison with major competitors."
  (4) Final output
  After completing the adjustments, save it as a standard industry Research Report to support corporate strategic decision-making.

## 8.3 Industry Risk Assessment (Example: Financial Industry Trend Analysis)

- Core Function
  DeepSeek integrates financial industry data, industry competition information, and policy environment to generate comprehensive industry trend Research Report, helping investors assess market opportunities and potential risks.
- Operation Detailed Steps
  (1) Data collection
  Compile market data and policy updates related to financial industry trends.
  (2) Generate a draft
  Prompt example: "Please generate a draft trend Research Report on the 'financial industry,' including market status, competitive landscape, policy environment, major risks, and investment recommendations. The text should be objective, data should be detailed, and charts should be included for clarification."

(3) Feedback and adjustments
Additional prompts: "Please provide a detailed description of financial market volatility, policy changes, regulatory uncertainties surrounding digital currencies, and the innovations and challenges brought by fintech in the risk assessment section, and conduct a detailed comparison with major competitors (e.g., leading banks and fintech companies)."

(4) Final output
After adjustments, the report will include a standardized format financial industry trend Research Report.

## 8.4 Market Outlook and Trend Analysis (Example: Stock Market Index Evaluation)

- Core Function
  Through DeepSeek's data analysis capabilities, users can comprehensively interpret market trends, macroeconomic indicators, and market hotspots, evaluate market trends, and provide forward-looking references for investment decisions.
- Operation Detailed Steps
  (1) Data input
  Compile macroeconomic data, stock index trends, major news, and market hotspot information.
  (2) Generate draft
  Prompt example: "Please generate a draft of the '2024 First Half Market Trend Research Report,' which should include market trends, macroeconomic environment, hotspot sector analysis, and risk warnings. The language should be standardized, data support should be sufficient, and line charts and pie charts should be embedded for explanation."
  (3) Feedback and optimization
  If more detailed data explanations are needed, add the instruction: "Please include specific growth data and future trend projections in the hot sector section."
  (4) Final draft
  After adjustments are made, generate the report for investors to reference.

## 8.5 Quantitative Trading Strategy Development (Example: Python Quantitative Trading Code Generation)

- Core Function
  DeepSeek not only generates text reports but also supports the development of code frameworks for quantitative trading models. By integrating historical data and risk control strategies, users can build and validate personalized quantitative trading systems.
- Operation Detailed Steps
  (1) Strategy definition
  Define the quantitative trading strategy (e.g., trend following and mean reversion) and collect relevant historical data.
  (2) Generate code framework
  Prompt example: "Please generate a Python code framework for a quantitative trading model based on the trend-following strategy, including data preprocessing, signal generation, backtesting modules, and risk control measures, with detailed comments added."
  (3) Feedback and debugging
  Additional instructions: "Please add a moving average indicator to the signal generation section and include Sharpe ratio calculations in the backtesting module."
  (4) Model validation
  Import the generated code into a local development environment for testing, optimize parameters based on actual data, and continue until the model is stable and reliable.

# Chapter 9
# Advanced DeepSeek Features and Cross-Platform Applications

This chapter introduces the advanced cross-platform applications of DeepSeek, including its collaboration with tools such as Jimeng AI, Mermaid, and Xmind. It also explains how to optimize intelligent agent training using multiround feedback iteration. Through specific Operation Detailed Steps and intuitive prompt examples, readers will learn how to extend DeepSeek's capabilities to areas such as image generation, data visualization, and personalized agent construction, thereby achieving efficient intelligent creation in diverse application scenarios.

## 9.1 DeepSeek + Word: Efficiently Obtain Work Materials

- Function Overview
  The integration of DeepSeek with Word can significantly enhance work efficiency. DeepSeek provides powerful information retrieval capabilities, helping users quickly find relevant content from vast amounts of data. Word, on the other hand, offers flexible document editing and formatting features. By utilizing DeepSeek, users can efficiently obtain the required materials and then use Word for organization and editing, greatly reducing search and collation time, and boosting work efficiency.
- Operation Detailed Steps and Prompt Example
  Go to the DeepSeek official website and click [API Open Platform] in the top right corner:

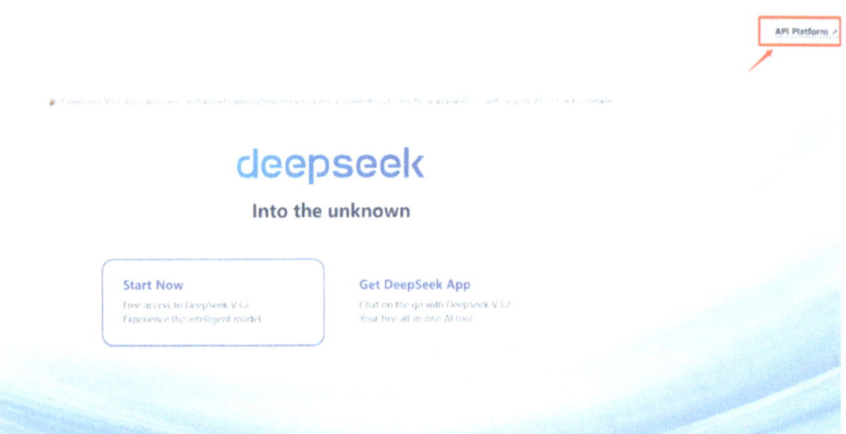


 | https://doi.org/10.1515/9783112218181-009

Click [API keys].

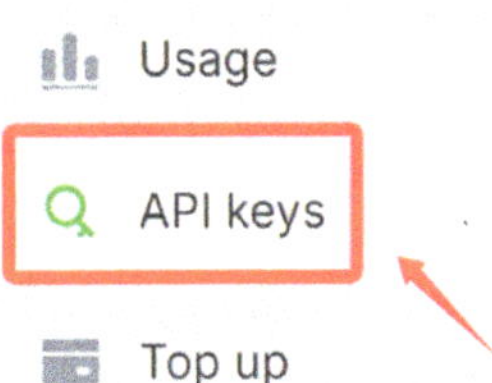


Click [Create API key], customize a name, and then create it:

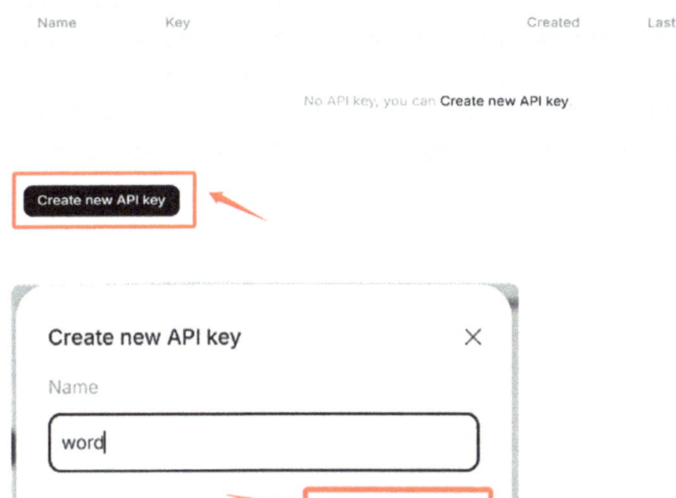

Create and generate the API key, copy it, and store it securely:

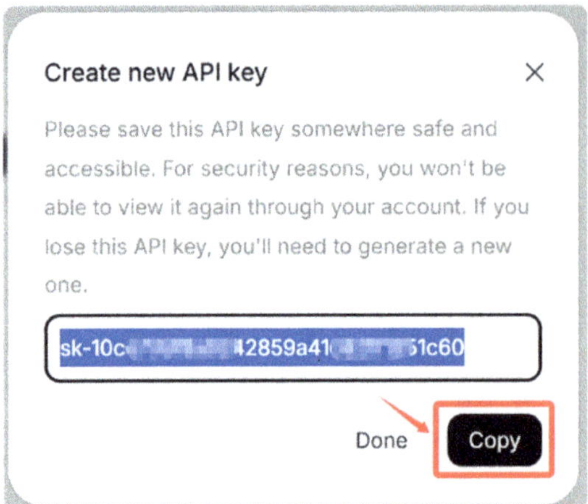


Click [File] > [Options] > [Trust Center] > [Trust Center Settings].

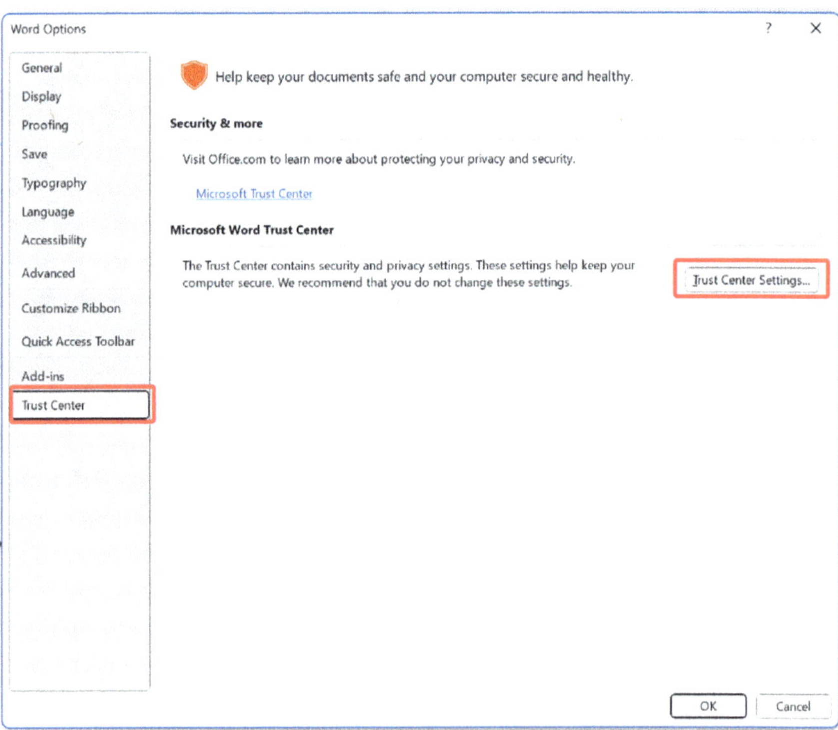

Under [Trust Center] > [Macro Settings], check [Enable all macros] and [Trust access to the VBA project object model], then click [OK]:

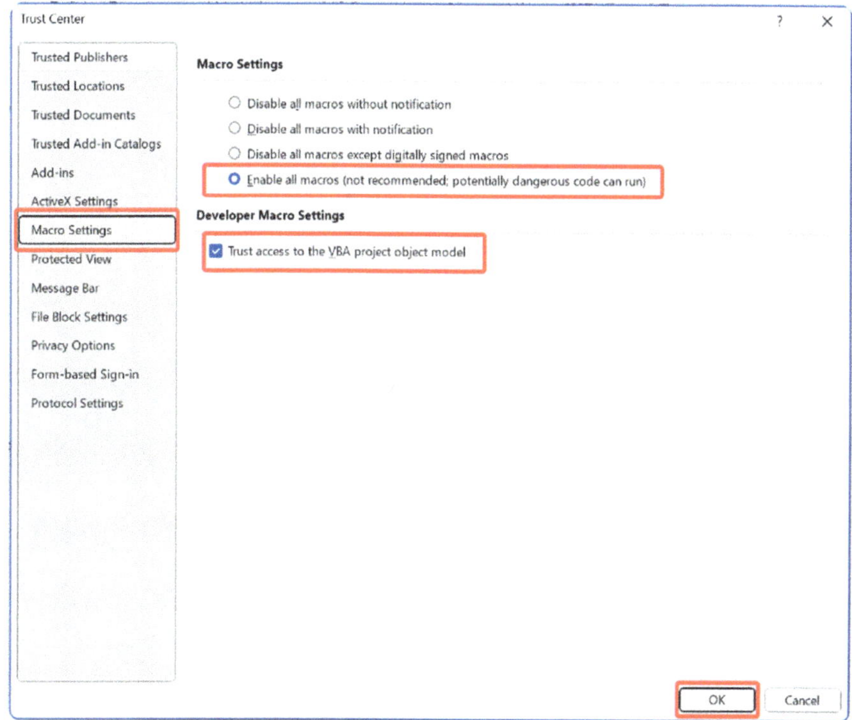

Open Word for configuration: Click [File] > [Options] > [Customize Ribbon] > [Main Tabs] and check the box for [Developer].

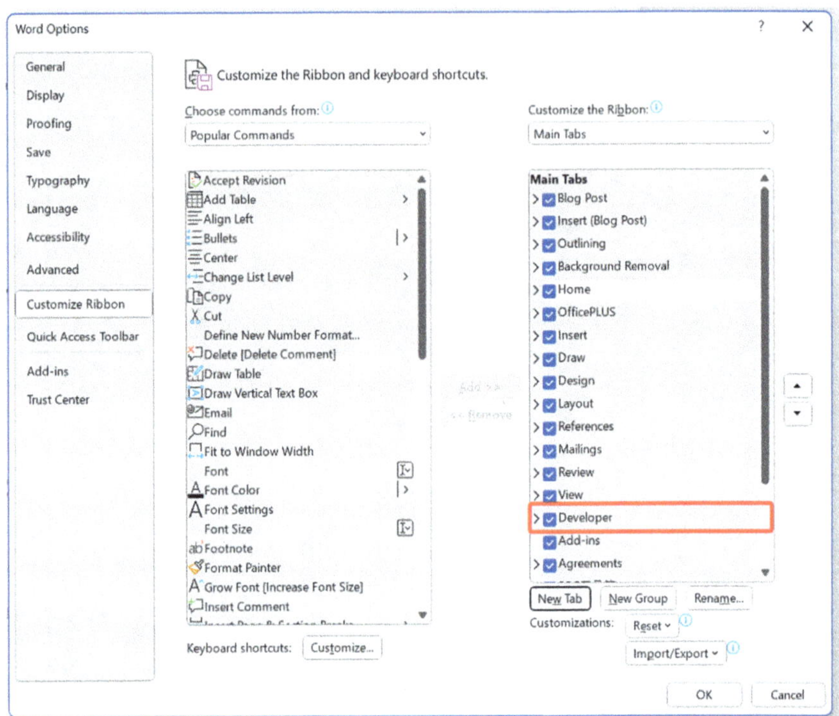


The [Developer] tab will now appear in the Word ribbon:

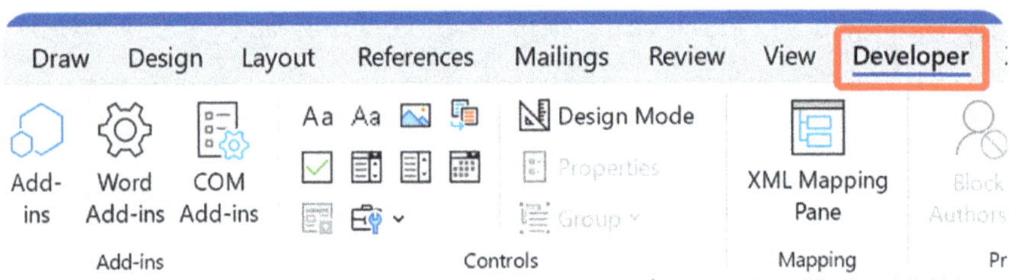

Click [Visual Basic] in the [Developer] tab:

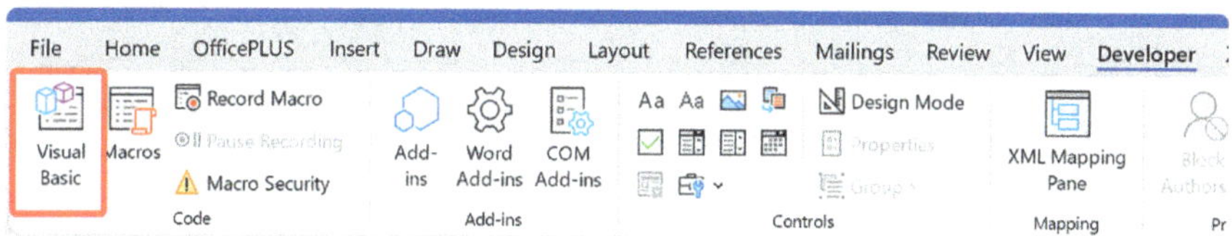


In the Visual Basic editor, select Insert > Module and paste the code (the code is open source at https://github.com/ProtoBeeCode/ai/blob/main/word). In the code, find API key = "您的API密钥" and replace "您的API密钥" with the API key you just created. Then close the editor:

```
Sub DeepSeekV3()
    Dim api_key As String
    Dim selectedText As String
    Dim userInput As String
    Dim finalInput As String
    Dim response As String
    Dim regex As Object
    Dim matches As Object
    Dim originalSelection As Range
    Dim inputResult As ModelSelection
    Dim modelType As String
    ' API Key
    api_key = "您的API密钥"
    If api_key = "" Then
        MsgBox "请输入API密钥。", vbExclamation
        Exit Sub
    End If
    ' 获取选中文本（如果有）
    If Selection.Type = wdSelectionNormal And Len(Selection.Text) > 0 Then
        selectedText = Selection.Text
        Set originalSelection = Selection.Range.Duplicate
    End If
    ' 显示自定义输入对话框
```

Configure the Word ribbon: Click [File] > [Options] > [Customize Ribbon] > [Developer] > [New Group (Custom)] and rename it:

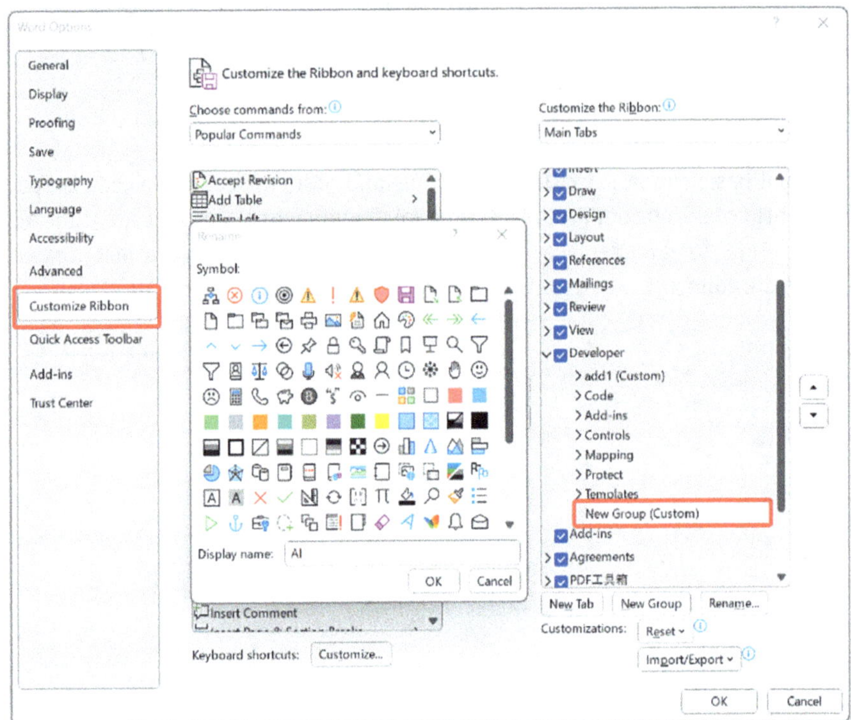

–> Under [Choose commands from:], select [Macros]. Add [Project.Module3.DeepSeekV3]. At this point, Word has been successfully connected to the DeepSeek large model.

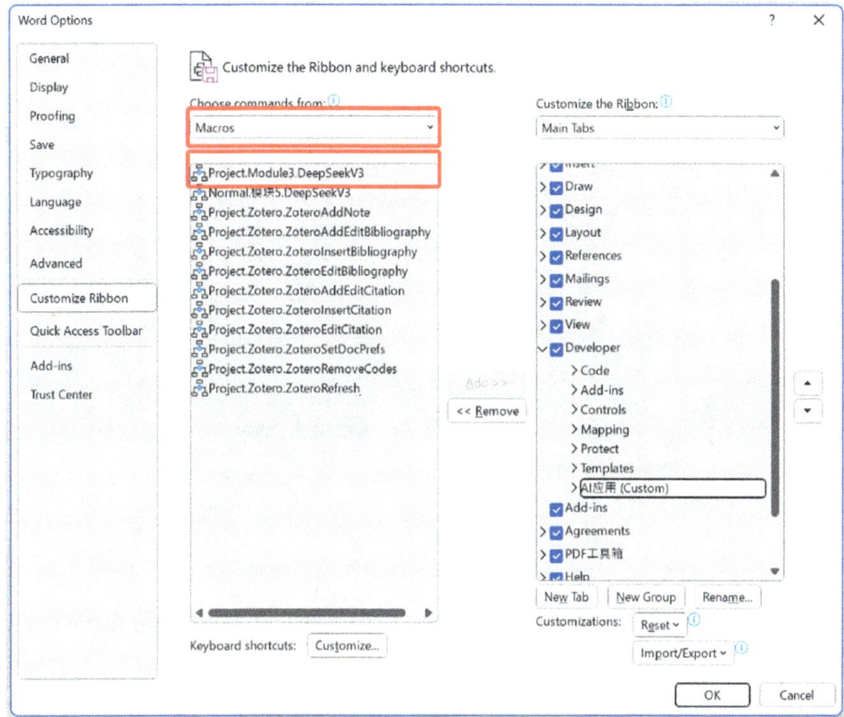

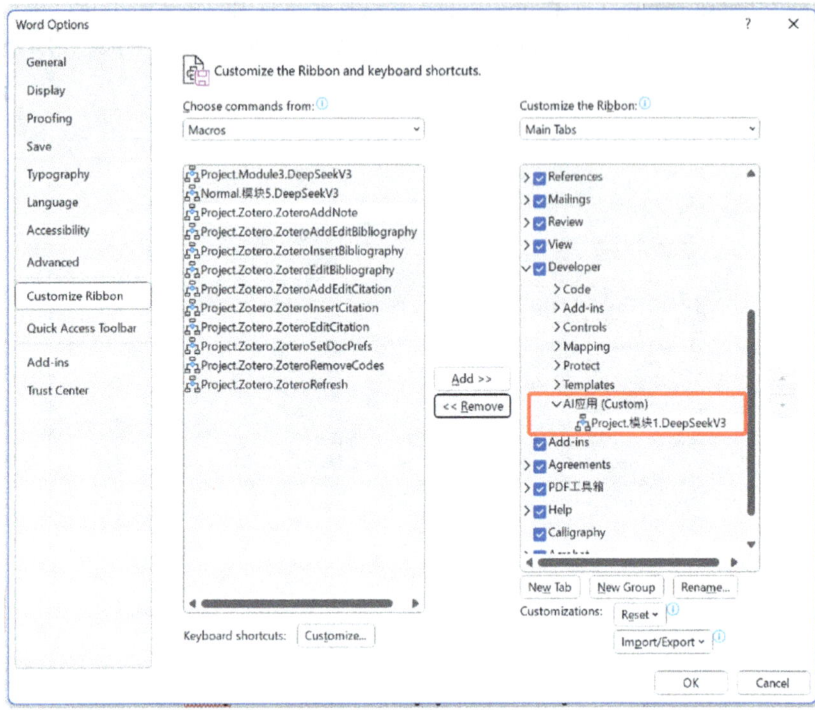


Click [Project.Module3.DeepSeekV3] under the [Developer] tab to start using the DeepSeek API settings:

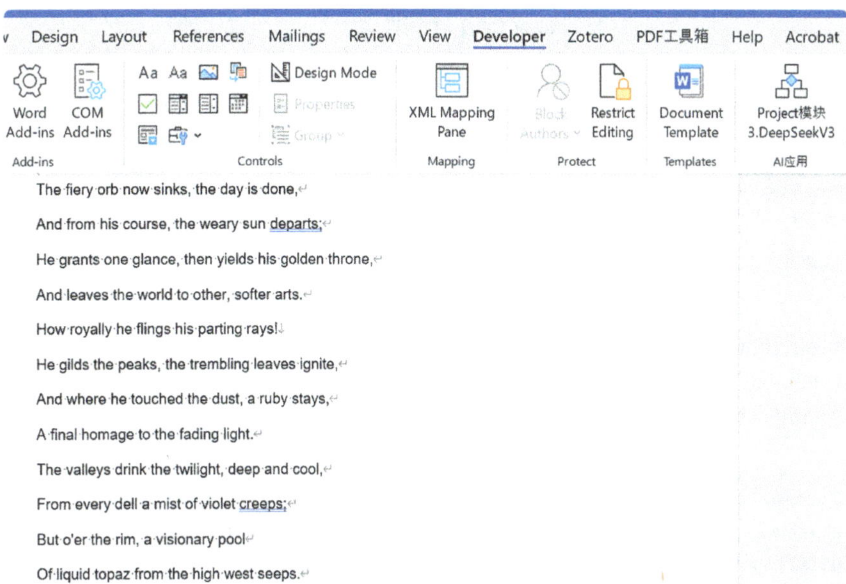


## 9.2 DeepSeek + Jimeng AI: Batch Generate High-Quality Posters

– Function Overview

Jimeng AI is a tool focused on image generation, creating high-quality images from text descriptions. The synergy between DeepSeek and Jimeng AI enables users to batch-generate visual materials that meet creative requirements, applicable in marketing, design, content creation, and other fields.

– Operation Detailed Steps and Prompt Example

(1) Input image description

First, use DeepSeek to generate a detailed image description. Prompt example:

"Task: Create a poster. You are an excellent senior graphic designer. Please help me design a Mid-Autumn Festival poster. It should feature mooncakes, have a main color scheme of red and gold, include a full moon hanging high, convey a Mid-Autumn Festival atmosphere, with the main text '喜迎中秋佳节' (Celebrating the Mid-Autumn Festival). It's for a social media poster. Please generate the Chinese AI painting prompt."

How can I help you?

Task: Create a poster. As an exceptionally skilled senior graphic designer, please design a Mid-Autumn Festival poster for me. It should feature moon cakes, primarily in red and gold tones, with a full moon prominently displayed to evoke the festive atmosphere. The main text should read "Celebrating the Mid-Autumn Festival." This poster is intended for use on social media. Please generate a Chinese AI art prompt for me.

DeepThink Search  

(2) Output image description

DeepSeek will generate the AI painting prompt based on the requirements, including scene composition and color matching:

A meticulously designed Mid-Autumn Festival poster, featuring traditional mooncakes as the central element, with exquisite patterns carved on the surface, enticing golden-yellow color, surrounded by traditional wooden mooncake molds. The background showcases a giant full moon, its soft light gently scattering over clouds, creating a rich festive atmosphere. The primary color palette uses red and gold, with red symbolizing celebration and joy, and gold representing harvest and prosperity. Traditional Chinese elements such as auspicious clouds, jade rabbits, and lanterns are integrated into the decorative patterns. The style is modern Chinese illustration with delicate lighting, rich layering, and intricate details, suitable for social media dissemination. The main text reads "Celebrating the Mid-Autumn Festival," presented in traditional calligraphy font with a three-dimensional gold effect, prominently placed in the golden ratio area of the composition.

(3) Import into Jimeng AI platform (https://jimeng.jianying.com/)

Open the Jimeng AI platform, click [图片生成], copy the generated AI painting prompt into the platform, set relevant parameters (e.g., resolution, style, and color tone), and start the generation function:

A meticulously designed Mid-Autumn Festival poster, featuring traditional mooncakes as the central element, with exquisite patterns carved on the surface, enticing golden-yellow color, surrounded by traditional wooden mooncake molds. The background showcases a giant full moon, its soft light gently scattering over clouds, creating a rich festive atmosphere. The primary color palette uses red and gold, with red symbolizing celebration and joy, and gold representing harvest and prosperity. Traditional Chinese elements such as auspicious clouds, jade rabbits, and lanterns are integrated into the decorative patterns. The style is modern Chinese illustration with delicate lighting, rich layering, and

 图片 4.1 1:1 高清 2K 

(4) Start generation function

(5) Adjustment and feedback

If some images are unsatisfactory, return to DeepSeek to adjust the description. Add instructions like: “Please optimize the description to add detailed descriptions of the characters.”

(6) Regenerate and export

Copy the adjusted image description back into the Jimeng AI platform, set parameters (e.g., resolution, style, and color tone), and start the generation function again. The final generated images can be saved as batch output files for use by marketing or design teams.

## 9.3 Mermaid + DeepSeek: Automated Flowchart Generation

– Function Overview
Mermaid is a text-based diagramming tool that generates flowcharts, sequence diagrams, and Gantt charts. By integrating with DeepSeek, users can directly convert text descriptions into professional charts, providing intuitive visual support for data analysis and project reporting.

– Operation Detailed Steps and Prompt Example
(1) Generate flowchart description and convert to Mermaid syntax
Input instruction in DeepSeek:

"Generate a flowchart description for a 'Product Development Process', covering stages like requirements research, prototype design, development testing, product release, and user feedback. Use arrows to represent flow relationships. Convert the description into Mermaid syntax code."

**How can I help you?**

Please generate a flowchart description for the "Product Development Process," covering the stages of requirement research, prototype design, development and testing, product release, and user feedback. Use arrows to indicate process relationships, and convert the flowchart description into Mermaid syntax.

DeepThink Search  

(2) Convert to Mermaid code

```
flowchart TD
    A[Requirements Gathering]
    B[Prototype Design]
    C[Development & Testing]
    D[Product Launch]
    E[User Feedback]

    A --> B
    B --> C
    C --> D
    D --> E
    E --> A
```

(3) Copy the code to Mermaid Live Editor
Real-time preview; adjust formats (e.g., node colors and font size).

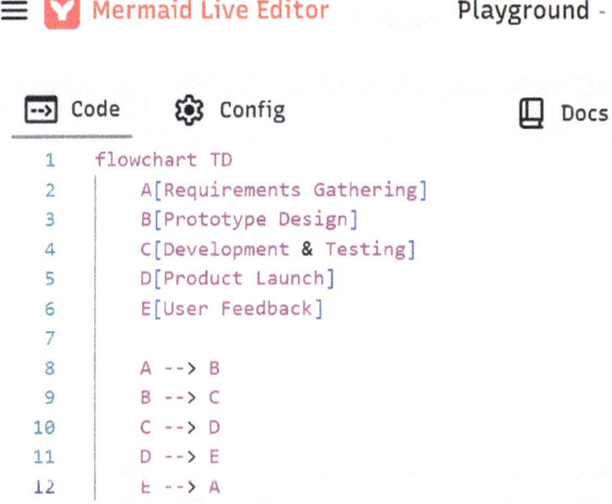

(4) Select export format
Choose PNG (high-resolution), SVG (editable vector), or PDF (document embedding):

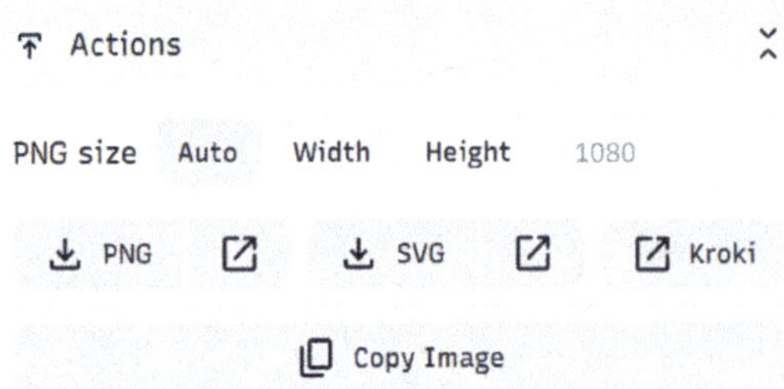


(5) Export chart.

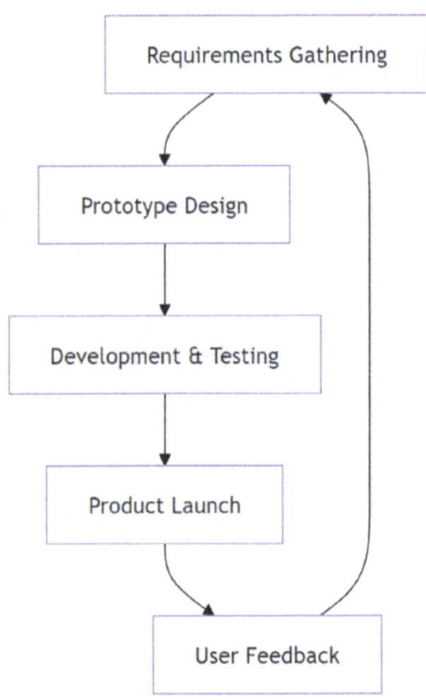


## 9.4 DeepSeek + Trello: AI-Powered Project Management

– Function Overview
The integration of DeepSeek and Trello combines artificial intelligence with project management. Leveraging DeepSeek's natural language processing and semantic parsing capabilities, it intelligently organizes and analyzes tasks. Users can input instruc-

tions in natural language, and DeepSeek automatically creates, categorizes, and updates Trello cards, ensuring clear project progress and rational task allocation. The system also provides intelligent suggestions based on historical data and trend analysis, optimizing project execution and enhancing team collaboration efficiency.

– Operation Detailed Steps and Prompt Example
(1) Generate task description and plan
Use DeepSeek to generate project task descriptions, progress reports, or plan outlines.
Prompt example:
"Generate a task outline for a 'New Product Promotion Plan', including task breakdown and key milestones. The outline will later be imported into a Trello board."

How can I help you?

Please generate a task outline for the "New Product Promotion Plan," which must include task breakdowns and key milestones. This task outline will subsequently be imported into the Trello board.

Search

**New Product Promotion Plan (Simple)**

**List 1: Strategy & Planning**

- **Card**: Define Goals, Target Audience, & Budget
- **Card**: Finalize Key Messaging & Launch Date
- **Card**: Set up Analytics & Tracking

**List 2: Content Creation**

- **Card**: Design Social Media Graphics & Ads
- **Card**: Write Website & Landing Page Copy
- **Card**: Prepare Launch Email & Blog Post
- **Card**: Create Press Kit & Product Photos

**List 3: Pre-Launch Buzz**

- **Card**: Teaser Campaign on Social Media
- **Card**: Build an Email Waitlist
- **Card**: Reach out to Influencers & Press

**List 4: Launch Day**

- **Card**: Publish Launch Announcements
- **Card**: Send Launch Email to List
- **Card**: Turn on Paid Ad Campaigns
- **Card**: Monitor Channels & Engage

**List 5: Post-Launch Review**

- **Card**: Analyze Performance Data
- **Card**: Gather Customer Feedback
- **Card**: Report on Results & Learnings

(2) Create Trello workspace
Open Trello (https://trello.com/) and create a new board:

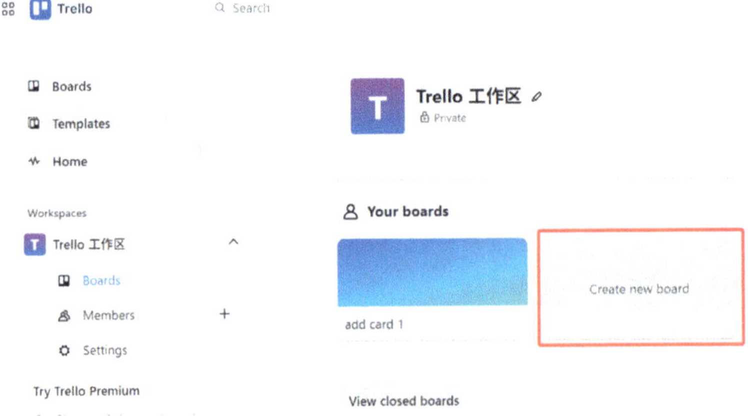

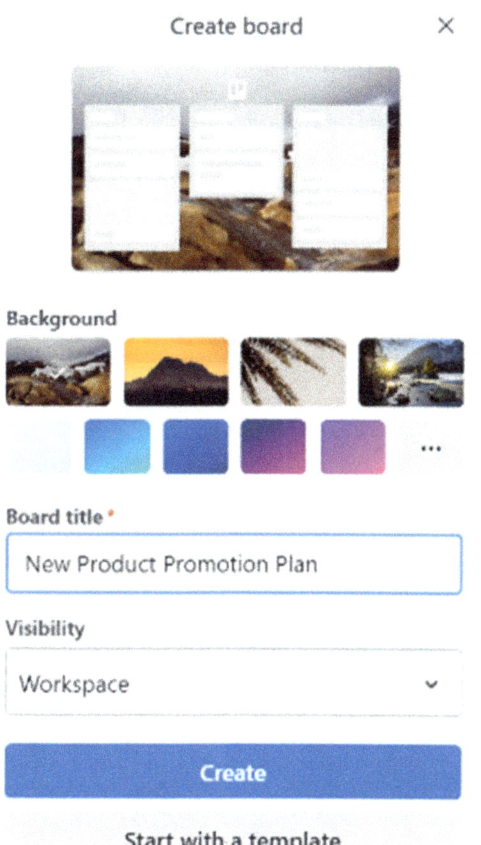


(3) Create task cards
Allocate the project task descriptions generated by DeepSeek into the Trello board, creating individual task cards:

New Product Promotion Plan

Strategy & Planning
Define Goals, Target Audience, Budget
Finalize Key Messaging & Launch Date
Set up Analytics & Tracking
+ Add a card

Content Creation
Design Social Media Graphics & Ads
Write Website & Landing Page Copy
Prepare Launch Email & Blog Post
Create Press Kit & Product Photos
+ Add a card

Pre-Launch Buzz
Teaser Campaign on Social Media
Build an Email Waitlist
Reach out to Influencers & Press
+ Add a card

Launch Day
Publish Launch Announcements
Send Launch Email to List
Turn on Paid Ad Campaigns
Monitor Channels & Engage
+ Add a card

Post-Launch Review
Analyze Performance Data
Gather Customer Feedback
Report on Results & Learnings
+ Add a card

(4) Optimize task descriptions and progress
Use optimization prompts like “Task decomposition” or “Progress tracking” to adjust task descriptions and ensure information accuracy.

(5) Regularly update and adjust task progress
Periodically update the Trello board, adjusting task progress based on feedback output by DeepSeek to achieve efficient project management.

## 9.5 DeepSeek + Napkin: Create Advanced Charts in 30 s

– Function Overview
DeepSeek is a deep search engine primarily used to extract valuable information from massive datasets. It supports multiple data sources and efficient retrieval.
Napkin is an open-source, lightweight note-taking application focused on simplicity and quick recording. It is suitable for both team collaboration and personal use, supporting rich text formatting and embedded media files.
Integration value: By combining DeepSeek and Napkin, users can achieve efficient data search and note organization, significantly enhancing information acquisition and collation efficiency.

– Operation Detailed Steps and Prompt Example
Open DeepSeek and input a query, e.g.:
“Outline the development of AI in various fields over the past 5 years in bullet points (≤100 words).

How can I help you?

Please outline the development of AI across various fields over the past five years. Keep it within 100 words.

Use the generated content as a design description:

Key Application Areas
- Education: Adaptive learning systems, AI tutoring
- Agriculture: Precision agriculture, yield forecasting
- Energy: Smart grid management, climate modeling
- Healthcare: Clinical decision support, drug development
- Computer Vision: Autonomous driving systems, facial recognition
- Industrial Applications: Predictive analytics, supply chain optimization, fintech, smart manufacturing

Copy the generated text.
Open Napkin (https://app.napkin.ai/) → Click 【 + New Napkin】 → Paste the content.

Hover to the left of the text: a lightning bolt icon will appear → click it to instantly generate multiple creative templates:

Key Application Areas

● Education: Adaptive learning systems, AI tutoring
Agriculture:Precision agriculture,yield forecasting
●Energy:Smart grid management,climatemodeling
● Healthcare: Clinical decision support, drug development
● Computer Vision: Autonomous driving systems,facial recognition
● Industrial Applications: Predictive analytics, supply chain optimization, fintech, smart manufacturing

Based on the thumbnails in the dropdown form, select a suitable style:

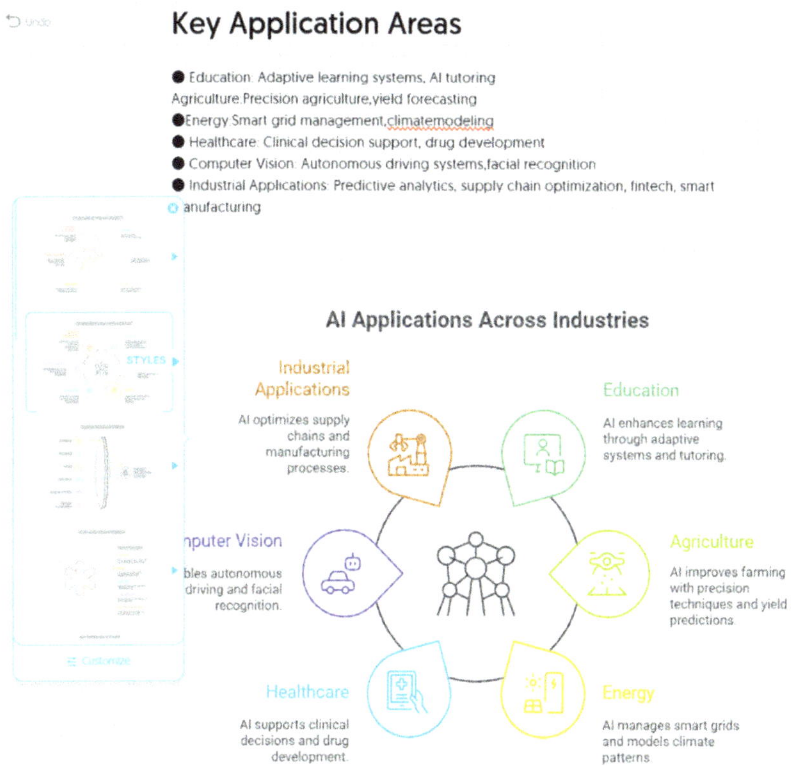

Select a suitable style → double-click icons or text to edit further:

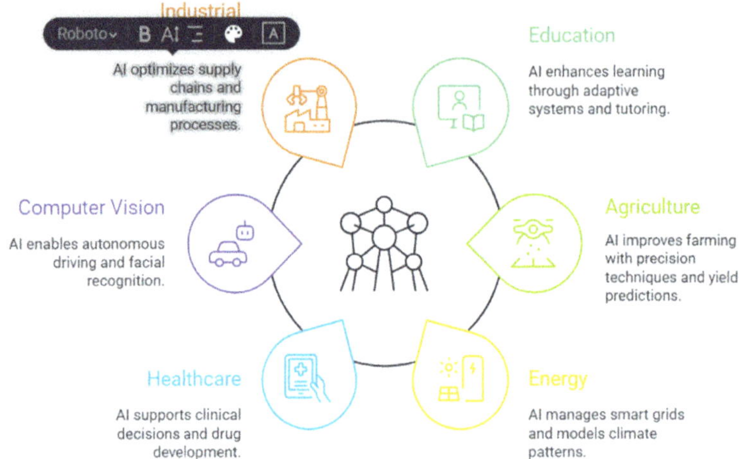

After editing, click the download icon (top right corner) → select export format: PNG, SVG, PDF, or PPT:

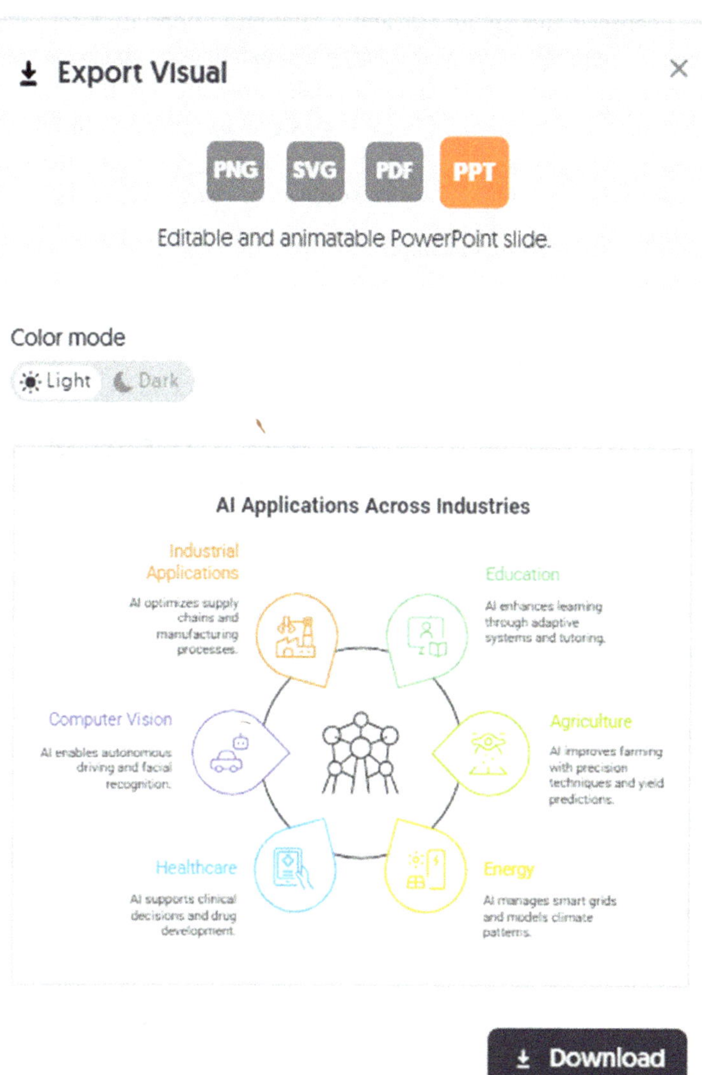

## 9.6 DeepSeek + Xmind: Automated Mind Map Generation

– Function Overview
The integration of DeepSeek and Xmind efficiently combines information retrieval with mind mapping. DeepSeek provides precise search capabilities to quickly extract relevant content from vast data, while Xmind visually presents this information through clear mind maps. Users can build knowledge structure diagrams in Xmind, leveraging DeepSeek's results to achieve rapid information organization, analysis, and visualization – enhancing work efficiency and decision-making capabilities.

– Operation Detailed Steps and Prompt Example
Upload file to DeepSeek

How can I help you?

Upload the file and send the command "I need to generate a mind map from the document content. Please deliver it in Formats recognized by X Mind." to DeepSeek:

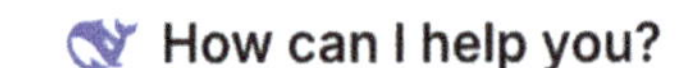


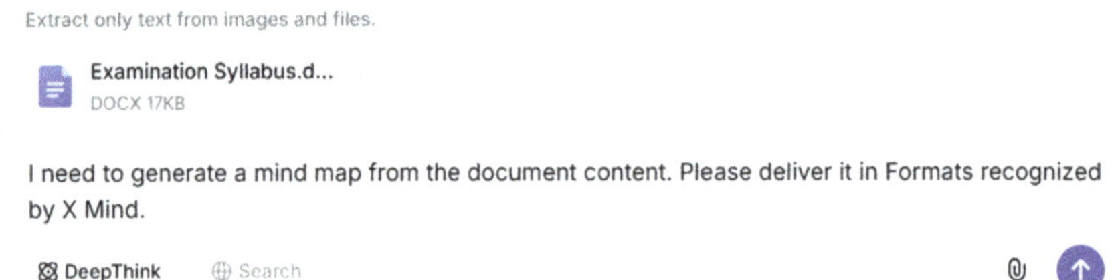

Generate mind map statements in OPML format compatible with Xmind:

```
<?xml version="1.0" encoding="UTF-8"?>
<opml version="1.0">
<head>
<title>Python Examination Syllabus</title>
</head>
<body>
<outline text="Python Examination Syllabus">

  <outline text="I. Python Fundamentals and Applications">
    <outline text="1. Evolution of Python Language"/>
    <outline text="2. Characteristics of Python Language"/>
    <outline text="3. Basic Programming Techniques">
      <outline text="• Code Indentation"/>
      <outline text="• Naming Conventions"/>
      <outline text="• Foundational Syntax"/>
    </outline>
    <outline text="4. Development Environment Setup">
      <outline text="• Python Interpreter Installation"/>
      <outline text="• Environment Configuration"/>
    </outline>
    <outline text="5. Simple Program Development">
      <outline text="• Comments"/>
      <outline text="• Naming & Reserved Words"/>
      <outline text="• Strings"/>
      <outline text="• Assignment Statements"/>
      <outline text="• Core Elements Practice"/>
    </outline>
  </outline>

  <outline text="II. Python Syntax Fundamentals">
    <outline text="1. Control Statements & Keywords">
      <outline text="• while, if, for loops"/>
      <outline text="• break, continue"/>
    </outline>
    <outline text="2. String Manipulation">
```

Create a new Microsoft Word document:

Right-click to view the document properties, change the extension from ".txt" to ".opml", and then confirm (Windows users need to disable "Hide known file extensions" in File Explorer):

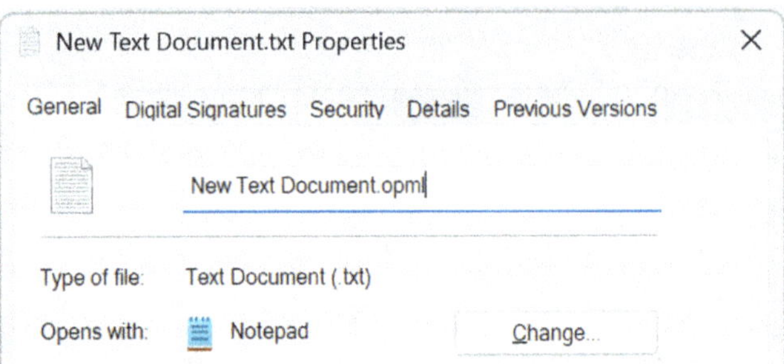


Paste the previously generated Xmind-recognizable mind map format statements into the "New Text Document.opml" file and save it.

Open Xmind, click [File] – [Import] – [Markdown], select "New Text Document. Opml," and confirm. Xmind will generate a logical mind map:

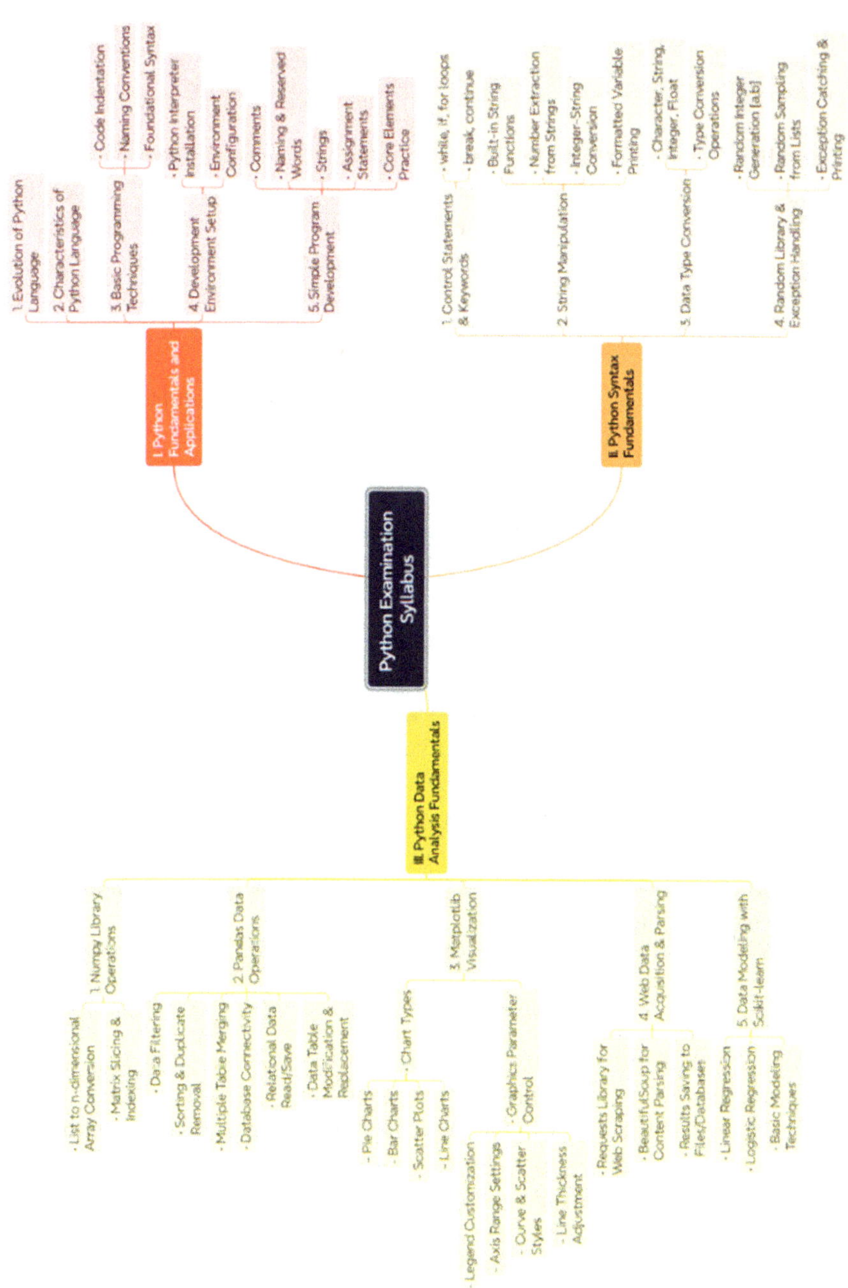
Python Examination Syllabus
I. Python Fundamentals and Applications
1. Evolution of Python Language
2. Characteristics of Python Language
3. Basic Programming Techniques
· Code Indentation
· Naming Conventions
· Foundational Syntax
4. Development Environment Setup
· Python Interpreter Installation
· Environment Configuration
5. Simple Program Development
· Comments
· Naming & Reserved Words
· Strings
· Assignment Statements
· Core Elements Practice
II. Python Syntax Fundamentals
1. Control Statements & Keywords
· while, if, for loops
· break, continue
2. String Manipulation
· Built-in String Functions
· Number Extraction from Strings
· Integer-String Conversion
· Formatted Variable Printing
3. Data Type Conversion
· Character, String, Integer, Float
· Type Conversion Operations
4. Random Library & Exception Handling
· Random Integer Generation [a,b]
· Random Sampling from Lists
· Exception Catching & Printing
III. Python Data Analysis Fundamentals
1. Numpy Library Operations
· List to n-dimensional Array Conversion
· Matrix Slicing & Indexing
2. Pandas Data Operations
· Data Filtering
· Sorting & Duplicate Removal
· Multiple Table Merging
· Database Connectivity
· Relational Data Read/Save
· Data Table Modification & Replacement
3. Matplotlib Visualization
· Chart Types
· Pie Charts
· Bar Charts
· Scatter Plots
· Line Charts
· Graphics Parameter Control
· Legend Customization
· Axis Range Settings
· Curve & Scatter Styles
· Line Thickness Adjustment
4. Web Data Acquisition & Parsing
· Requests Library for Web Scraping
· BeautifulSoup for Content Parsing
· Results Saving to Files/Databases
5. Data Modeling with Scikit-learn
· Linear Regression
· Logistic Regression
· Basic Modeling Techniques

# Chapter 10
# Future Outlook and Continuous Innovation

At a time when digitalization and intelligent transformation are accelerating, artificial intelligence technology is reshaping industries at an unprecedented pace. As a leading Chinese large language model, DeepSeek excels not only in text generation, intelligent Q&A, and data analysis but also demonstrates significant potential in cross-platform integration, industrial applications, and personalized services. This chapter will explore DeepSeek's potential future expansions across various fields, its technological evolution, and its profound impact on socioeconomic development. It will also analyze the challenges and opportunities it faces, providing readers with insights for continuous innovation and strategic planning.

## 10.1 Deep Learning and Large Model Technology: Emerging Trends

### 10.1.1 Technological Evolution and Breakthroughs

In recent years, driven by enhanced computing power and expanded data scale, deep learning and large-scale model technologies have achieved significant breakthroughs. DeepSeek, based on the Transformer architecture and trained on massive corpora, delivers highly accurate and fluent outputs in Chinese natural language processing. Looking ahead, with more efficient algorithms and advanced hardware, DeepSeek is poised to continuously upgrade in model precision, response speed, and multimodal data processing capabilities.

### 10.1.2 Cross-Domain Integration Trends

Future AI models will extend beyond single-task applications, with cross-domain integration becoming mainstream. DeepSeek is actively exploring deep convergence with technologies such as image generation, speech recognition, and knowledge graph construction to achieve "multimodal" intelligent interaction, providing users with comprehensive solutions. For example, through integration with tools such as Jimeng AI and Mermaid, DeepSeek generates visually enhanced reports and presentations, offering intuitive data support for business decision-making and marketing.

 | https://doi.org/10.1515/9783112218181-010

## 10.2 Future Prospects and Continuous Innovation

### 10.2.1 Education Sector

In education, DeepSeek serves as an intelligent learning assistant, helping teachers generate lesson plans, knowledge summaries, and grade assignments, while supporting students in self-directed learning. As demand for personalized learning grows, DeepSeek will optimize educational content through data feedback, enabling tailored teaching approaches. For instance, teachers use DeepSeek to create lecture notes, review outlines, and practice question banks, while students receive customized learning advice via conversational interactions.

### 10.2.2 Healthcare Sector

DeepSeek assists in generating medical reports, case analyses, and research paper abstracts, while enabling doctors to access clinical advice through intelligent Q&A. With the digitization of medical data and the rise of telemedicine, DeepSeek will enhance diagnostic efficiency and decision support. For example, doctors leverage DeepSeek to summarize medical records, interpret complex clinical guidelines, and integrate imaging data via cross-platform tools for precise diagnosis.

### 10.2.3 Finance and Investment Sector

Amid rapidly changing financial markets, DeepSeek automates stock analysis, industry evaluations, and market trend forecasts, aiding investors in developing scientific quantitative trading strategies. As financial data integration and AI algorithms advance, DeepSeek's applications in finance will become more accurate and efficient. Investors utilize it to generate predictive reports, compare historical and real-time data for decision-making, and build personalized strategies through quantitative trading modules.

## 10.3 Continuous Innovation and Social Impact

### 10.3.1 Continuous Optimization and Feedback Mechanisms

DeepSeek's strength lies in its iterative feedback mechanism. As user data accumulates, the system continuously refines its algorithms to improve accuracy and adaptability. This self-learning capability ensures that DeepSeek maintains technological leadership.

### 10.3.2 Socioeconomic and Enterprise Transformation

AI is reshaping global economies and business operations. DeepSeek, as an efficient tool, helps enterprises reduce costs, enhance productivity, and drive digital transformation. Its adoption also spurs innovation across industries, impacting employment, industrial structures, and governance. For example, companies deploy DeepSeek for smart office solutions, digital marketing, and data-driven decisions, boosting competitiveness and high-quality development.

## 10.4 Challenges and Opportunities

### 10.4.1 Technological Breakthroughs and Market Demand

With ongoing advances in computing resources and algorithms, future DeepSeek models will support more complex scenarios while meeting growing demands for personalized, precise services.

### 10.4.2 Data Privacy and Ethical Security

Large-scale data applications necessitate stringent data privacy and AI ethics. DeepSeek must comply with evolving regulations, requiring enterprises to strengthen security mechanisms and balance innovation with social responsibility.

# Appendix A: 100 AI Writing Prompts and Optimization Tips for Multi-scenario Applications

This appendix contains 100 prompt examples and optimization tip examples, covering government documents and business documents, as well as fields such as education, social media, technology, and analysis.

## Government Document Writing (30 Prompts)

1. Government work report drafting
Prompt example:
"Generate a draft 2024 Government Work Report with sections: 'Achievements,' 'Problems,' 'Improvement Measures,' and 'Future Plans.' Use formal language with concrete data."
Optimization tip:
Verify data accuracy; append "Include statistical data in the 'Problems' section."

2. Government work report: content expansion
Prompt example:
"Expand the 'Problems' section in the 2024 Government Work Report with detailed analysis of public safety risks and economic downturn trends, supported by cited data from NBS (National Bureau of Statistics)."
Optimization tip:
Verify data sources and precision; require hyperlinks to official databases.

3. Department work report drafting
Prompt example:
"Generate a draft 2024 Marketing Department Annual Report with sections: Work Review, KPIs, Issues, and Improvement Suggestions. Use bullet points with YoY comparison charts."
Optimization tip:
Embed dynamic Excel tables for real-time data updates.

4. Detailed supplement to departmental work report
Prompt example:
"Please supplement the report with key performance metrics from the past three years."
Optimization tip:
Embed dynamic Excel tables for real-time data updates.

 | https://doi.org/10.1515/9783112218181-011

5. Policy implementation report
Prompt example:
"Draft a National Safety Directive Implementation Report with: Directive Summary, Execution Status (list measures with responsible units), Issues, and Rectification Plans."
Optimization tip:
Apply RACI Matrix (Responsible-Accountable-Consulted-Informed) in execution details.

6. Refinement of implementation reporting
Prompt example:
"Please add rectification progress and specific quantitative metrics in the execution status section, and clarify responsibility assignments in the improvement measures."
Optimization tip: Ensure improvement measures specify responsible persons/roles.

7. Draft generation of project report
Prompt example:
"Generate a draft of the 'Smart Logistics Project Progress Report' covering project background, implementation progress, achievements demonstration, existing issues, and follow-up plans."
Optimization tip: Suggest incorporating data charts in the achievements demonstration.

8. Data chart supplement for project report
Prompt example:
"Please generate a line chart illustrating key achievements in the results section, highlighting trends in major metrics."
Optimization tip: Verify consistency between charts and textual descriptions.

9. Work report draft generation
Prompt example:
"Generate a draft of the Quarterly Work Report with sections for achievements, issues, and future plans. Use bullet points and maintain objective language."
Optimization tip: Incorporate key performance indicator (KPI) data.

10. Work report data optimization
Prompt example:
"Add specific KPI metrics and historical comparison charts to the work report."
Optimization tip: Ensure data charts are clear and accurate.

11. Research report draft generation
Prompt example:
"Generate a draft of the Regional Digital Economy Research Report covering market status, competitive analysis, existing issues, and policy recommendations. Use objective language and substantiate with data."
Optimization tip: Detail competitor data in the competitive analysis section.

12. Research report chart integration
Prompt example:
"Incorporate market share and growth rate charts into the research report to visualize data trends."
Optimization tip: Verify standardized chart annotations.

13. Issue research report draft generation
Prompt example:
"Generate a draft of the Internal Communication Barriers Research Report, including background, current analysis, root causes, and improvement suggestions."
Optimization tip: Add case studies to the root cause analysis.

14. Issue research report case refinement
Prompt example:
"Supplement the root cause analysis with real cases and statistical data."
Optimization tip: Ensure logical alignment between cases and data.

15. Rectification report draft generation
Prompt example:
"Generate a draft of the Work Safety Rectification Report, detailing measures, expected outcomes, responsibilities, and timelines. Use formal language and data support."
Optimization tip: Specify deadlines and inspection criteria for each measure.

16. Rectification report refinement optimization
Prompt example:
"Expand each measure with specific implementation plans and follow-up monitoring protocols."
Optimization tip: Set measurable targets for plans and protocols.

17. Learning reflection report generation
Prompt example:
"Generate a draft of the National AI Forum Learning Reflection Report, summarizing content, personal insights, and improvement suggestions. Use sincere and fluent language."
Optimization tip: Include recommendations for future learning.

18. Learning reflection report content supplement
Prompt example:
"Add case studies and self-reflection sections to the learning report."
Optimization tip: Maintain clear content hierarchy.

19. Project proposal draft generation
Prompt example:
"Generate a draft of the Smart Manufacturing Project Proposal, covering background, objectives, implementation plan, budget, and expected benefits. Use concise language with data support."
Optimization tip: Detail risk control measures in the implementation plan.

20. Project proposal risk refinement
Prompt example:
"Include specific risk assessments and mitigation strategies in the implementation plan."
Optimization tip: Ensure risk controls are actionable.

21. Generic work summary report generation
Prompt example:
"Generate a generic Department Work Summary Report outlining key achievements, issues, and improvements. Present in bullet points."
Optimization tip: Structure into "Achievements," "Issue Analysis," and "Future Planning."

22. Generic work summary report format optimization
Prompt example:
"Optimize the Work Summary Report structure with section headings and bullet-point lists."
Optimization tip: Maintain consistent formatting.

23. Speech draft generation
Prompt example:
"Generate a draft speech on 'Corporate Culture Development,' covering core principles, success cases, and future outlook (≥150 words per section)."
Optimization tip: Add data to success cases.

24. Speech language optimization
Prompt example:
"Enhance the speech's emotional impact and conclude with an inspiring call to action."
Optimization tip: Ensure consistent language style.

25. Party-building document draft generation
Prompt example:
"Generate a draft of the Party Organization and Ideological Work Report, including review, experience summary, issues, and improvements. Use rigorous language."
Optimization tip: Highlight Party principles and outcomes in the experience summary.

26. Party-building document content supplement
Prompt example:
"Please add specific success cases and party member activity data in the Party-building report."
Optimization tip: Ensure the cases are representative and the data is authentic.

27. Government correspondence proposal generation
Prompt example:
"Please generate a draft of the 'Annual Enterprise Proposal,' which should include project background, proposal text, and resolution recommendations. The language should be formal and the structure clear."
Optimization tip: Add specific discussion points in the proposal text.

28. Government correspondence proposal refinement
Prompt example:
"Please add data support and detailed reasons for resolutions in the proposal section."
Optimization tip: Ensure arguments are sufficient and logic is clear.

29. Request document generation
Prompt example:
"Generate a draft of the Request for Increased R&D Investment, detailing rationale, expected benefits, and risk controls."
Optimization tip: Add background context and specific figures.

30. Approval document generation
Prompt example:
"Generate a draft of the Approval for Increased R&D Investment Request, including approval feedback and next Detailed Steps. Use formal language."
Optimization Tip: Ensure wording reflects approval hierarchy.

## 20 Business and Workplace Document Writing Commands

1. Business email drafting
Prompt example:
"Please generate a draft of a business email for 'Confirmation of Cooperation Intent,' which should include background of both parties, cooperation content, cooperation terms, and follow-up plans. The language should be polite and formal."
Optimization tip: Add specific cooperation details, such as scheduling and contact information.

2. Internal notice generation
Prompt example:
"Please generate a draft of a 'Department Meeting Notice,' which should specify the meeting time, location, agenda, and participation requirements. The format should be standardized and the language concise."
Optimization tip: Suggest adding a clear agenda and a method for confirming attendance.

3. Automated meeting minutes organization
Prompt example:
"Please generate a draft of the 'Department Quarterly Meeting Minutes,' which should be divided into 'Discussion Points,' 'Decision Results,' and 'Follow-up Actions.' The language should be formal."
Optimization tip: Clarify the division of responsibilities and timeframes in the 'Follow-up Actions' section.

4. Work daily report writing
Prompt example:
"Please generate a draft of the 'Work Daily Report,' which should include completed tasks, existing problems, and tomorrow's plan, presented in bullet points."
Optimization tip: Suggest adding specific task completion details and improvement measures.

5. Project plan report generation
Prompt example:
"Please generate a draft of the '2025 Annual Marketing Promotion Plan,' which should be divided into goal setting, strategy deployment, execution Detailed Steps, and evaluation metrics."
Optimization tip: Clarify tasks and budget allocations for each stage in the execution Detailed Steps.

6. Resume generation and optimization
Prompt example:
"Please generate a draft resume that includes personal basic information, work experience, and project experience. The language should be concise and the structure reasonable."
Optimization tip: Add specific achievements and numerical indicators in the project experience section.

7. Job application letter writing
Prompt example:
"Please generate a draft job application letter for a digital marketing position, highlighting personal strengths and relevant experience."
Optimization tip: Emphasize job motivation and alignment with company culture.

8. Business proposal report generation
Prompt example:
"Please generate a draft of the 'New Product Marketing Promotion Plan,' which should include market research, competition analysis, promotion strategies, and budget allocation."
Optimization tip: Ensure logical coherence between sections, and add specific execution Detailed Steps in the promotion strategies.

9. Generate investment research report
Prompt example:
"Generate a draft of 'Emerging Industry Investment Research Report', covering market opportunities, potential risks, SWOT analysis, and investment recommendations."
Optimization tip:
"Detail market challenges and countermeasures in the SWOT analysis section."

10. Write performance evaluation report
Prompt example:
"Generate a draft of 'Department Quarterly Performance Evaluation Report', listing key performance indicators (KPIs), year-over-year data, and improvement suggestions."
Optimization tip:
"Add charts to visualize performance data."

11. Generate PPT outline
Prompt example:
"Generate a PPT outline on 'Digital Transformation Strategy', including main sections, key data, and chart descriptions."
Optimization tip:
"Ensure the outline is well-structured and comprehensively covers the topic."

12. Draft meeting speech
Prompt example:
"Draft a speech on 'Corporate Culture Development', covering introduction, core arguments (≥150 words per section), and conclusion."
Optimization tip:
"Incorporate real case studies and data in core arguments."

13. Business Proposal Writing
Prompt example:
"Draft a 'Cross-Border Collaboration Project Proposal', detailing collaboration background, project objectives, implementation plan, and expected benefits."
Optimization tip:
"Ensure the proposal has a complete structure and sufficient supporting evidence."

14. Organize customer communication records
Prompt example:
"Generate a summary of customer communication records, categorizing main discussion points, customer needs, and follow-up plans.
Optimization tip:
"Use bullet points to highlight key information and action items."

15. Generate market competition research report
Prompt example:
"Draft a 'Industry Competitive Landscape Research Report', including key competitors, market share, and future trend predictions."
Optimization tip:
"Conduct detailed SWOT analysis for each competitor (Strengths, Weaknesses, Opportunities, Threats)."

16. Create internal training materials
Prompt example:
"Generate content for an internal training course on 'Digital Transformation Fundamentals', requiring clear structure and comprehensive content."
Optimization tip:
"Attach practical case studies after each knowledge point to illustrate applications."

17. Draft performance improvement plan
Prompt example:
"Generate a 'Team Performance Improvement Plan' draft, covering problem diagnosis, improvement measures, and expected outcomes."
Optimization tip:
"Specify executable Detailed Steps for each measure (e.g., timelines, responsible parties)."

18. Generate business negotiation scripts
Prompt example:
"Create a set of business negotiation scripts for 'Price Negotiation', using precise and persuasive language suitable for face-to-face discussions."
Optimization tip:
"Include dialogue simulations to demonstrate real-world application."

19. Generate annual corporate work summary report
Prompt example:
"Draft a 'Corporate Annual Work Summary Report', listing yearly achievements, existing issues, and future plans in bullet points."
Optimization tip:
"Ensure department-specific data is clearly quantified."

20. Draft strategic planning proposal
Prompt example:
"Generate a 'Corporate Future Strategic Plan Proposal', divided into current status analysis, strategic goals, implementation roadmap, and risk management measures."
Optimization tip:
"Define phased milestones with measurable KPIs."

## 20 AI Writing Prompts for Education and Learning

1. Course design plan generation
Prompt example:
"Please generate a draft of the Fundamentals of Artificial Intelligence Course Design Plan, including course objectives, syllabus, and assessment methods."
Optimization tip: Add specific teaching cases and a resource list.

2. Teaching case report generation
Prompt example:
"Please generate a draft of the Case Study Report on University AI Courses, describing the case background, implementation outcomes, and improvement suggestions."
Optimization tip: Refine case data and clarify conclusions.

3. Assignment grading feedback report
Prompt example:
"Please generate a feedback report on High School English Essay Grading, pointing out major issues and giving improvement suggestions."
Optimization tip: Clearly define grading standards and scoring criteria.

4. Study plan development
Prompt example:
"Please generate a draft of a Self-study AI Learning Plan for College Students, divided into short-, mid-, and long-term goals, with specific learning content."
Optimization tip: Add time schedules and recommended resources under each goal.

5. Knowledge preview summary generation
Prompt example:
"Please generate a preview summary on Fundamentals of Deep Learning, covering core concepts, main algorithms, and application scenarios."
Optimization tip: Ensure concise language and highlight key points.

6. Research paper outline generation
Prompt example:
"Please generate an outline for a paper on Applications of Machine Learning in Finance, including background, methodology, data, and expected results."
Optimization tip: Add detailed subtopics to each section.

7. Review content generation
Prompt example:
"Please generate a Study Guide on Core AI Concepts, covering basic terminology, key algorithms, and representative cases."
Optimization tip: Enhance retention using charts or mind maps.

8. Chinese-English translation practice
Prompt example:
"Please translate the following Chinese passage into standard American English, keeping professional terminology and formal tone."
Optimization tip: Check grammar and consistency of technical terms.

9. Learning reflection writing
Prompt example:
"Please generate a draft of a Learning Reflection Report on Attending an AI Forum, summarizing key content, personal insights, and improvement suggestions, in a sincere and fluent style."
Optimization tip: Add future applications and improvement ideas.

10. Exam question generation
Prompt example:
"Please generate 5 multiple-choice questions with answers on Fundamentals of Deep Learning, covering beginner to intermediate levels."
Optimization tip: Ensure coverage of core knowledge points.

11. Lecture slide outline generation
Prompt example:
"Please generate an outline for Frontier Technologies in AI, including main knowledge points and discussion questions."
Optimization tip: Add supporting cases and data after each point.

12. Academic paper abstract writing
Prompt example:
"Please generate an abstract for a paper on Image Recognition Algorithms, ensuring precise language and comprehensive information."
Optimization tip: Cover research methods and key conclusions.

13. Lab report template generation
Prompt example:
"Please generate a Deep Learning Experiment Report template, including objectives, methodology, data analysis, and conclusion."
Optimization tip: Remind users to add specific experimental data.

14. Seminar outline generation
Prompt example:
"Please generate an outline for a seminar on AI Ethics and Social Impacts, divided into background, key issues, and discussion recommendations."
Optimization tip: Add relevant cases and references.

15. Online tutoring Q&A set generation
Prompt example:
"Please generate a Q&A set on Machine Learning Model Tuning, covering common questions and key answers."
Optimization tip: Ensure clear structure and specific questions.

16. Educational case sharing report
Prompt example:
"Please generate a draft Smart Classroom Practice Case Report, describing the implementation process, problems encountered, and improvements."
Optimization tip: Add real data and teacher feedback.

17. Academic conference paper title generation
Prompt example:
"Please generate 5 paper titles on AI and Data Mining, concise and attractive."
Optimization tip: Ensure coverage of core issues.

18. Academic collaboration proposal writing
Prompt example:
"Please generate a draft of a Cross-university Research Collaboration Proposal, including background, research content, expected outcomes, and collaboration method."
Optimization tip: Describe the collaboration model in detail.

19. Learning resource recommendation list
Prompt example:
"Please generate an AI Learning Resources Recommendation list with 5 quality online courses and books, each with a brief introduction."
Optimization tip: Ensure diversity, covering both basics and advanced materials.

20. Professional skills test generation
Prompt example:
"Please generate 5 test questions with answers on Python Programming, from beginner to intermediate level."
Optimization tip: Cover all key knowledge areas and provide detailed explanations.

## 20 AI Writing Prompts for Creative Content and Social Media

1. Creative short video script outline
Prompt example:
"Please generate an outline for a short video on Green Technology, including opening, theme presentation, interaction, and closing call-to-action."
Optimization tip: Add specific questions for audience interaction.

2. Social media article drafting
Prompt example:
"Please generate a draft article on Future Cities, with vivid language, unique perspectives, and supporting data."
Optimization tip: Add specific cases and charts to improve persuasiveness.

3. Creative title generation
Prompt example:
"Please generate 10 creative titles on Smart Homes, each within 12 words, concise and powerful."
Optimization tip: Ensure alignment with the topic and audience interest.

4. Modern poetry creation
Prompt example:
"Please generate a modern poem on The Digital Age, with at least 4 lines per stanza, fresh language, and rhythm."
Optimization tip: Adjust rhythm for smooth poetic flow.

5. Novel opening generation
Prompt example:
"Please generate the opening of a sci-fi novel on Transformations in the Future World, with engaging plot and strong setup."
Optimization tip: Strengthen background and character motivation.

6. Video script detailing
Prompt example:
"Please generate a detailed script for a short video on Smart Wearables, including setting, dialogues, and scene descriptions."
Optimization tip: Ensure logical flow and audience engagement.

7. Interactive social copywriting
Prompt example:
"Please generate 5 social media posts on Environmental Initiatives, fun and engaging to spark discussion."
Optimization tip: Add concrete interaction questions or calls to action.

8. Brand story writing
Prompt example:
"Please generate a brand story on Technological Innovation, covering founder background, growth, and future vision."
Optimization tip: Include data and success cases.

9. Creative advertising copywriting
Prompt example:
"Please generate 5 creative ads on Green Energy, each under 12 words."
Optimization tip: Ensure alignment with brand tone and adjust style as needed.

10. Image + text social media article
Prompt example:
"Please generate a draft social article on Future Lifestyles, with clear structure, integrating text and visuals."
Optimization tip: Add chart explanations and image suggestions.

11. Short video hosting script
Prompt example:
"Please generate a draft hosting script for a short video on Technology Changing Life, with natural and inspiring language."
Optimization tip: Add interactive Q&A at opening and closing.

12. Radio program script
Prompt example:
"Please generate a draft script for a radio show on Opportunities in Digital Transformation, including opening, discussion, and closing remarks."
Optimization tip: Ensure major viewpoints are covered vividly.

13. Creative title list generation
Prompt example:
"Please generate 10 creative titles on AI Innovation, short and impactful."
Optimization tip: Ensure close alignment with the theme.

14. Social media interview questions
Prompt example:
"Please generate a set of interview questions on Future Work Models, covering trends, challenges, and opportunities."
Optimization tip: Add targeted questions for multiple perspectives.

15. Cultural commentary writing
Prompt example:
"Please generate a commentary draft on Fusion of Traditional Culture and Modern Technology, with plain language and unique insights."
Optimization tip: Add concrete examples and supporting data.

16. Internet buzzword analysis article
Prompt example:
"Please generate a draft article analyzing an Internet Buzzword, explaining its origin and social impact in lively language."
Optimization tip: Ensure clarity and logical rigor.

17. Video voiceover script
Prompt example:
"Please generate a voiceover script on The Digital Future, with vivid imagery and emotional tone."
Optimization tip: Adjust pacing and tone for appeal.

18. Product review writing
Prompt example:
"Please generate a draft product review on Smart Home Devices, describing pros, cons, user experience, and suggestions."
Optimization tip: Add specific usage data and consumer feedback.

19. Lifestyle blog post
Prompt example:
"Please generate a draft blog post on Healthy Eating, with scientific data and real cases, in a friendly tone."
Optimization tip: Ensure representative data and vivid language.

20. Emotional story writing
Prompt example:
"Please generate a draft of an emotional story about 'Growth and Struggle,' requiring a deeply moving plot and sincere, touching language."
Optimization tip: It is recommended to add detailed descriptions and emotional fluctuations in the story.

## 10 Technical Assistance and Data Analysis Application Commands

1. Code generation
Command example: "Please use Python to generate a code snippet that calculates the average of a list and add detailed comments."
Optimization tip: Check the code logic and handle exceptions properly.

2. Code debugging guidance
Command example: "Please generate a guide on 'Code Debugging,' listing common errors and debugging techniques."
Optimization tip: Ensure the guide covers multiple debugging scenarios.

3. Data chart generation
Command example: "Please generate a draft report on 'Sales Data Trends,' embedding line charts and pie charts, and provide chart explanations."
Optimization tip: Ensure the data sources are clear and the charts are visually appealing.

4. API documentation writing
Command example: "Please generate a draft of the 'DeepSeek API Interface Documentation,' detailing each API's function, parameters, and return formats."
Optimization tip: Check the document structure to ensure clarity and organization.

5. Technical blog article generation
Command example: "Please generate a draft of a technical blog article on 'Applications of Transformer Models in NLP,' ensuring the language is concise and technically sound."
Optimization tip: Include specific examples and experimental data in the article.

6. System performance optimization report
Command example: "Please generate a draft report on 'How to Optimize AI Model Performance,' including data processing, model tuning, and hardware recommendations."
Optimization tip: Ensure the report has a complete structure and add practical application cases.

7. Test case generation
Command example: "Please generate 5 Python test cases on 'Data Preprocessing,' covering common error scenarios and providing reference answers."
Optimization tip: Ensure the test cases cover all major scenarios.

8. Model training process documentation
Command example: "Please generate a draft technical document on the 'DeepSeek Model Training Process,' describing data preprocessing, model training, and validation Detailed Steps."
Optimization tip: Ensure the Detailed Steps are detailed and logically organized.

9. Exception handling code example
Command example: "Please generate a Python code snippet showing how to catch and handle exceptions during data processing, with detailed comments."
Optimization tip: Ensure code robustness and provide clear exception explanations.

10. Technical white paper outline generation
Command example: "Please generate an outline for a white paper on 'Practical Applications of AI Models in Business,' including background, methodology, case analysis, and future outlook."
Optimization tip: Add specific examples and supporting data in each section to ensure content depth and richness.

# Appendix B: 30 Cross-Industry Practical Application Cases

This appendix contains practical application cases from 30 different industries. Each case includes a specific scenario description, detailed operation Detailed Steps, the feedback and iteration process, as well as optimization suggestions. Following each case, there are 20 diversified instruction optimization recommendations, aimed at helping you continuously improve based on feedback when using DeepSeek for official document drafting, text optimization, and decision support, thereby enhancing output quality.

## Case 1: Legal – Drafting a Commercial Contract

- Scenario
  A well-known tech company plans to sign a long-term strategic cooperation agreement with an overseas supplier. To ensure the rights and obligations of both parties are clearly defined, a law firm is tasked with drafting a detailed commercial contract.
- Detailed Steps:
  1. Initial draft: Input instruction: "Please draft a '2024 Annual Commercial Contract' including both parties' basic information, transaction terms, breach of contract liability, and dispute resolution mechanisms, written in precise legal language and standard format."
  2. First draft review: The "breach of contract liability" clause is too vague and lacks specific penalties.
  3. Feedback for revision: Additional instruction: "Please add specific penalties and a compensation calculation formula to the 'breach of contract liability' section, and change the basic information section into a table format."
  4. Multiple feedback rounds: Further refine clause wording and formatting.
  5. Final output: A clear, detailed, data-supported draft commercial contract.
- Prompt Optimization Suggestions:
  1. Use precise, unambiguous legal expressions.
  2. Specify breach of contract clauses.
  3. Standardize compensation formulas.
  4. Present key information in tables.
  5. Ensure clear division of responsibilities.
  6. Use authoritative legal terminology.
  7. Maintain strict logical coherence.
  8. Support clauses with sufficient data.
  9. Provide thorough risk warnings.

 | https://doi.org/10.1515/9783112218181-012

10. Use bullet points.
11. Cite the latest laws and regulations.
12. Ensure consistent formatting.
13. Keep language objective and neutral.
14. Maintain clear paragraphing and transitions.
15. Include explicit penalty descriptions.
16. Ensure a consistent document style.
17. Support with examples.
18. Add annotations for key clauses.
19. Ensure legal liability descriptions are accurate.
20. Compare with industry-standard contract templates.

## Case 2: Education – Designing a University Course Plan

- Scenario:
  A well-known university plans to launch an "Introduction to Artificial Intelligence" course. A detailed course design plan is needed to meet curriculum reform requirements and enhance students' practical skills.
- Detailed Steps:
  1. Initial draft: Input instruction: "Please draft a 'Course Design Plan for Introduction to Artificial Intelligence' including course objectives, syllabus, main content, and assessment methods."
  2. First draft review: Some syllabus descriptions are not detailed enough.
  3. Feedback for revision: Additional instruction: "Please add detailed case discussions and practical sessions in the syllabus section, and list reference textbooks."
  4. Multiple feedback rounds: Refine assessment methods, adding grading criteria for lab sessions.
  5. Final output: A complete, well-structured, practical course design plan.
- Prompt Optimization Suggestions:
  1. Clearly define course objectives.
  2. Structure syllabus logically.
  3. Include case discussions for each module.
  4. Describe practical sessions in detail.
  5. Ensure scientific, reasonable assessment methods.
  6. Provide accurate textbook references.
  7. Use bullet points for clarity.
  8. Balance theory and practice.
  9. Include interactive teaching designs.
  10. Emphasize innovation and practicality.
  11. Support arguments with sufficient data and examples.

12. Keep expressions concise and impactful.
13. Cover both foundational and advanced topics.
14. Ensure the structure fits teaching logic.
15. Use professional terms with explanations.
16. Make teaching design actionable.
17. Increase student engagement.
18. Include clear timelines.
19. Provide detailed grading rubrics.
20. Include feedback and improvement mechanism

## Case 3: Publishing – Editing Review Report

- Scenario:
  A publisher receives a new manuscript. An editor must write a review report evaluating structure, language fluency, and logical consistency, and provide revision suggestions for the author.
- Detailed Steps:
  1. Initial draft: Input instruction: "Please draft a 'New Manuscript Review Report' including language fluency, structural soundness, logical consistency, and improvement suggestions."
  2. First draft review: Some paragraphs have weak logical connections.
  3. Feedback for revision: Additional instruction: "Identify logical gaps in the report, suggest specific revisions, and recommend transitional words to improve flow."
  4. Multiple feedback rounds: Add concrete rewrite examples.
  5. Final output: A detailed review report with actionable feedback.
- Prompt Optimization Suggestions:
  1. Ensure smooth, coherent language.
  2. Clearly mark logical gaps.
  3. Recommend transitional words.
  4. Provide actionable revision suggestions.
  5. Use consistent formatting.
  6. Offer multiple rewrite examples.
  7. Ensure data accuracy.
  8. Keep tone objective and rigorous.
  9. Highlight key points in bullet form.
  10. Maintain consistent style.
  11. Add charts or visuals when relevant.
  12. Provide detailed, specific examples.
  13. Keep language concise and logical.
  14. Ensure clear structure.

15. Emphasize practical value.
16. Provide ample correction examples.
17. Explain technical terms clearly.
18. Ensure smooth paragraph transitions.
19. List improvements step-by-step.
20. Focus on final quality enhancement.

## Case 4: New Media – Creative Article Writing

- Scenario:
  A new media studio plans a creative article about "Future Cities," requiring unique perspectives, engaging language, and strong brand messaging.
- Detailed Steps:
  1. Initial draft: Input instruction: "Please draft a creative article about 'Future Cities' with vivid language, unique viewpoints, and relevant data support."
  2. First draft review: Content is too basic and lacks innovation.
  3. Feedback for revision: Additional instruction: "Add innovative perspectives combining future technology and urban planning, and include specific data and case studies."
  4. Multiple feedback rounds: Adjust tone to be more persuasive.
  5. Final output: A creative, data-rich, engaging article.
- Prompt Optimization Suggestions:
  1. Present unique, forward-looking viewpoints.
  2. Include detailed, relevant data.
  3. Use lively, innovative language.
  4. Provide vivid, concrete examples.
  5. Keep writing engaging and captivating.
  6. Use vivid metaphors.
  7. Maintain persuasive tone.
  8. Organize ideas clearly.
  9. Add interactive questions.
  10. Use keywords like "future technology" and "urban innovation."
  11. Highlight market trend analysis.
  12. Reference authoritative data.
  13. Use short, punchy sentences.
  14. Keep wording concise.
  15. Use catchy titles.
  16. Include user case studies.
  17. Infuse emotional resonance.
  18. Ensure smooth viewpoint transitions.
  19. Add interactive discussion prompts.

20. Use keywords like "resonance" and "innovative perspective."

## Case 5: Food and Beverage – Menu Copy and Promotional

- Scenario:
  A well-known restaurant chain launches a new "Healthy Meal" and needs copywriting for menus and a promotional announcement.
- Detailed Steps:
  1. Initial draft: Input instruction: "Please draft menu copy and a promotional announcement for a 'New Healthy Meal,' including dish descriptions, nutritional info, and promotion details, with friendly, enticing language."
  2. First draft review: Dish descriptions and promotion details lack specificity.
  3. Feedback for revision: Additional instruction: "Add detailed ingredient and cooking method descriptions to the 'dish description' section, and specify promotion time, discount details, and participation conditions in the announcement."
  4. Multiple feedback rounds: Enhance appeal with more emotional language.
  5. Final output: Well-formatted, detailed, lively menu copy and promotional announcement.
- Prompt Optimization Suggestions:
  1. Provide detailed dish descriptions.
  2. Ensure ingredient accuracy.
  3. Describe cooking methods vividly.
  4. Specify promotion details.
  5. Quantify discount rates.
  6. Provide precise promotion timing.
  7. List participation conditions.
  8. Use warm, inviting language.
  9. Add comforting vocabulary.
  10. Use creative titles.
  11. Include customer feedback.
  12. Use bullet points.
  13. Ensure data reliability.
  14. Emphasize brand image.
  15. Use keywords like "healthy" and "nutritious."
  16. Keep tone lively.
  17. Add keywords like "fresh," "trendy," and "tempting."
  18. Be concise and direct.
  19. Maintain clear structure.
  20. Add promotional incentives.

## Case 6: Cross-Border Trade – Export Contract Drafting

- Scenario:
  A cross-border trade company signs an export agreement with an overseas client. The legal department must draft a detailed export contract.
- Detailed Steps:
  1. Initial draft: Input instruction: “Please draft an ‘Export Contract’ including both parties’ details, product specifications, pricing terms, payment methods, and dispute resolution mechanisms, in formal language and standard format.”
  2. First draft review: Pricing terms are too vague.
  3. Feedback for revision: Additional instruction: “Add a detailed calculation formula and exchange rate explanation in the ‘pricing terms’ section, and specify delivery time and logistics responsibilities.”
  4. Multiple feedback rounds: Add breach of contract and compensation clauses.
  5. Final output: A clear, internationally compliant export contract.
- Prompt Optimization Suggestions:
  1. Specify pricing terms clearly.
  2. Standardize exchange rate explanations.
  3. Provide exact delivery dates.
  4. Clarify logistics responsibilities.
  5. Detail breach of contract liability.
  6. Make compensation calculations transparent.
  7. Use international contract standards.
  8. Ensure natural logical flow.
  9. Maintain strict data accuracy.
  10. Use standard tables.
  11. Ensure professional terminology is correct.
  12. Cover all risk warnings.
  13. Use bullet points for key clauses.
  14. Cite legal sources.
  15. Keep document style consistent.
  16. Be concise and precise.
  17. Balance rights and obligations.
  18. Include “force majeure” clauses.
  19. Pay attention to detail.
  20. Add keywords like “international standards” and “legal review.”

## Case 7: E-commerce – Product Page Copywriting

- Scenario:
  An e-commerce platform launches a new “Smart Home Speaker” and needs compelling product page copy.
- Detailed Steps:
  1. Initial draft: Input instruction: “Please draft product page copy for a ‘Smart Home Speaker’ including features, technical specs, usage scenarios, and customer reviews, with concise and persuasive language.”
  2. First draft review: Technical specs are vague; usage scenarios lack detail.
  3. Feedback for revision: Additional instruction: “Add details such as power, sound quality, and compatibility in the ‘technical specs’ section, and describe typical household usage scenarios.”
  4. Multiple feedback rounds: Add real customer review data.
  5. Final output: A data-rich, well-structured product page.
- Prompt Optimization Suggestions:
  1. Describe product features specifically.
  2. Provide detailed technical specs.
  3. Make usage scenarios vivid.
  4. Use real customer reviews.
  5. Support with sufficient data.
  6. Keep language concise and persuasive.
  7. Match brand tone.
  8. Use visual aids.
  9. Maintain logical flow.
  10. Keep tone professional yet friendly.
  11. Highlight competitive advantages.
  12. Use keywords like “positive reviews” and “real experience.”
  13. Break structure into sections.
  14. Keep tone lively.
  15. Ensure keyword accuracy.
  16. Add product comparisons.
  17. Make wording easy to understand.
  18. Use data charts for clarity.
  19. Highlight innovation.
  20. Add keywords like “smart,” “convenient,” and “leading.”

## Case 8: FMCG – New Product Promotion Announcement

- Scenario:
  An FMCG brand launches a new healthy drink and needs a promotion announcement to quickly capture market attention.
- Detailed Steps:
  1. Initial draft: Input instruction: "Please draft a promotional announcement for a new healthy drink, including product highlights, promotion details, and discount policies, with concise and powerful language."
  2. First draft review: Promotion details are unclear.
  3. Feedback for revision: Additional instruction: "List promotion time, discount rates, participation conditions, and add ingredient and health benefit descriptions to the 'product highlights' section."
  4. Multiple feedback rounds: Adjust tone to be more modern and persuasive.
  5. Final output: A detailed, data-supported, engaging promotion announcement.
- Instruction Optimization Suggestions:
  1. "Promotion details should be described clearly."
  2. "Event duration must be specified precisely."
  3. "Quantify the discount magnitude clearly."
  4. "List participation requirements one by one."
  5. "Highlight product features with specific ingredients/components."
  6. "Use language that is highly persuasive/compelling."
  7. "Adopt a stylish, modern tone."
  8. "Ensure that all data citations are accurate."
  9. "Include keywords such as 'limited-time offer' and 'buying frenzy.'"
  10. "Keep the style lively yet professional."
  11. "Make the wording concise and forceful."
  12. "Tighten sentence structures for a compact flow."
  13. "Emphasize maximizing consumer benefits."
  14. "Use motivational calls to action."
  15. "Consider using animated charts for support."
  16. "Balance the tone appropriately."
  17. "Consider adding user experience feedback."
  18. "Maintain a strong overall rhythm in the copy."
  19. "Add keywords like 'fresh' and 'best-seller.'"
  20. "Use words such as 'innovative,' 'intuitive,' and 'enticing.'"

## Case 9: Tourism – Travel Guide Generation

- Scenario:
  Scenario: A travel company aims to promote Guilin tourism by providing visitors with a detailed and practical travel guide, including scenic spot introductions, itinerary planning, transportation guidance, and local food recommendations.
- Detailed Steps:
  1. Initial generation: Input instruction. "Please generate a draft travel guide for a Guilin landscape tour, including scenic spot introductions, itinerary planning, transportation guidance, and food recommendations, with vivid language."
  2. First presentation: The scenic spot introduction is relatively brief.
  3. Feedback modification: Add instruction. "Please expand the 'Scenic Spot Introduction' section with detailed historical and cultural background and recommended tour routes. Also, supplement the 'Transportation Guidance' with shuttle bus information."
  4. Multiple rounds of feedback: Suggest adjusting the writing style to be more interactive and warm.
  5. Final output: Generate a richly illustrated, detailed, and friendly-toned travel guide.
- Instruction Optimization Suggestions:
  1. "Scenic spot descriptions should be vivid and specific."
  2. "Historical background should be introduced in detail."
  3. "Tour routes should be clearly planned."
  4. "Transportation information should be concrete and practical."
  5. "Food recommendations should highlight local specialties."
  6. "Language should be warm and interactive."
  7. "Use recommendation phrases such as 'must-visit' or 'not to be missed.'"
  8. "Incorporate local customs and cultural heritage during optimization."
  9. "Use data charts for intuitive presentation."
  10. "Adjust tone to be lively and friendly."
  11. "Include prompt words like 'enhanced experience.'"
  12. "Emphasize travel safety reminders."
  13. "Consider quoting visitor feedback."
  14. "Wording should be inspiring and appealing."
  15. "Ensure the structure is clearly divided into sections."
  16. "Word choice should be vivid and descriptive."
  17. "Suggest adding interactive Q&A sections."
  18. "Use expressions like 'in-depth experience.'"
  19. "Emphasize cultural depth."
  20. "Include prompt words like 'travel essentials' and 'unique experience.'"

## Case 10: Studying Abroad – Application Essay Writing

- Scenario: A study abroad consulting agency aims to improve students' admission success rates by drafting a personal statement for an outstanding student, emphasizing academic achievements and career planning.
- Detailed Steps:
  1. Initial generation: Input instruction. "Please generate a draft of a study abroad personal statement, covering personal background, academic achievements, motivation for studying abroad, and future plans. The language should be sincere and the logic clear."
  2. First presentation: The section on motivation for studying abroad is relatively vague.
  3. Feedback modification: Add instruction. "Please expand the 'Motivation for Studying Abroad' section by adding specific personal experiences and their connection to career planning. Describe the practical impact of studying abroad on future development."
  4. Multiple rounds of feedback: Further request to optimize overall logic and persuasiveness of the language.
  5. Final output: A comprehensive, logically rigorous, and sincerely written personal statement.
- Instruction Optimization Suggestions:
  1. "Motivation for studying abroad should be specific and vivid."
  2. "Personal experiences should be described in detail."
  3. "Academic achievements should highlight key strengths."
  4. "Logical structure should be rigorous and orderly."
  5. "Language should be sincere and touching."
  6. "Future plans should be emphasized clearly."
  7. "Use standardized professional terminology."
  8. "Consider adding successful case references."
  9. "Use comparisons to strengthen arguments."
  10. "Expression should be well-organized."
  11. "Use phrases such as 'enhancing study abroad competitiveness.'"
  12. "Data citations must be accurate."
  13. "Writing style should be formal yet approachable."
  14. "Emphasize rich practical experiences."
  15. "Language should be persuasive."
  16. "Use expressions such as 'clear future outlook.'"
  17. "Focus on detailed content."
  18. "Emphasize goal-oriented clarity."
  19. "Include career development planning."
  20. "Incorporate keywords such as 'competitive advantage,' 'academic background,' and 'future planning.'"

## Case 11: Financial Services – Investment Strategy Report Writing

- Scenario:
  A financial institution aims to guide investors by drafting an investment strategy report on emerging industries, covering market analysis and risk assessment.
- Detailed Steps:
  1. Initial generation: Input instruction. "Please generate a draft of the '2024 First Half Investment Strategy Report,' including market analysis, portfolio recommendations, and risk assessment. The language should be professional, and the data thorough."
  2. First presentation: The risk assessment section is insufficient.
  3. Feedback modification: Add instruction. "Please expand the 'Risk Assessment' section with specific risk response measures and comparative analysis using historical data. Strengthen forward-looking recommendations in the conclusion."
  4. Multiple rounds of feedback: Further request to optimize the overall structure of the report.
  5. Final output: Generate a well-structured investment strategy report with sufficient data support.
- Instruction Optimization Suggestions:
  1. "Risk assessment should be detailed and thorough."
  2. "Investment recommendations should be data-driven."
  3. "Structure should be clear and well-organized."
  4. "Language should remain objective and rational."
  5. "Recommend using historical data comparison."
  6. "Emphasize dynamic risk control."
  7. "Provide specific risk response strategies."
  8. "Suggest adding market trend forecasts."
  9. "Use expressions such as 'reasonable asset allocation.'"
  10. "Conclusion should be forward-looking and clear."
  11. "Use professional financial terminology."
  12. "Data charts should be visually intuitive."
  13. "Logical reasoning should be thorough and rigorous."
  14. "Recommend citing authoritative analytical data."
  15. "Expression should be clear and accurate."
  16. "Include optimization terms such as 'stable,' 'forward-looking,' and 'precise.'"
  17. "Emphasize investment portfolio optimization."
  18. "Recommend using strategic planning."
  19. "Wording should be concise and powerful."
  20. "Include keywords such as 'risk management,' 'market volatility,' and 'dynamic adjustment.'"

## Case 12: Healthcare – Clinical Case Report Generation

- Scenario:
  A top-tier hospital needs to write a clinical case report on cardiac interventional therapy for academic exchange and outcome evaluation. The report must be data-rich and comply with medical standards.
- Detailed Steps:
  1. Initial generation: Input instruction: "Please generate a draft of a 'Cardiac Interventional Therapy Case Report,' including case background, diagnostic process, treatment plan, and follow-up results. The language should be professional, and the data should be detailed."
  2. First output: Diagnostic process description is vague.
  3. Feedback and revision: Additional instruction:
     "Please add specific examination data and imaging descriptions in the 'Diagnostic Process' section, and refine the treatment plan."
  4. Multiple rounds of feedback: Requirement to supplement long-term follow-up data.
  5. Final output: Generate a detailed clinical case report that complies with medical standards.
- Instruction Optimization Suggestions:
  1. "Diagnostic process should be detailed and specific."
  2. "Examination data must be thorough."
  3. "Imaging descriptions should be precise and professional."
  4. "Follow-up results should include sufficient long-term data."
  5. "Use medical professional terminology."
  6. "Structure should comply with clinical report standards."
  7. "Language should remain objective and rigorous."
  8. "Data charts should visually present results."
  9. "Recommend citing authoritative medical literature."
  10. "Include clear pathological analysis during optimization."
  11. "Emphasize the rationality of the treatment plan."
  12. "Descriptions should be well-structured and hierarchical."
  13. "Language should be concise yet professional."
  14. "Recommend using standardized case report format."
  15. "Ensure risk warnings are sufficient."
  16. "Add explanations of diagnostic criteria."
  17. "Incorporate keywords such as 'clinical observation' and 'follow-up records.'"
  18. "Support with statistical data."
  19. "Provide comprehensive background information on the case."
  20. "Emphasize treatment outcome tracking."

## Case 13: Manufacturing – Production Process Optimization Plan

- Scenario:
  A manufacturing enterprise is facing low production efficiency and urgently needs to develop a production process optimization plan to reduce costs and improve efficiency through process reengineering.
- Detailed Steps:
  1. Initial generation: Input instruction. "Please generate a draft of the Production Process Optimization Plan, including descriptions of the current process, bottleneck analysis, optimization measures, and expected benefits. The language should be standardized and data detailed."
  2. First presentation: The "bottleneck analysis" section is not specific enough.
  3. Feedback modification: Add instruction.
     "Please include delay times and transportation cost analysis in the 'bottleneck analysis' section, and provide detailed descriptions of improvement measures and responsibility assignments."
  4. Multiple feedback iterations: Suggest adding quantitative indicators in the "expected benefits" section.
  5. Final output: Generate a production process optimization plan with a clear structure and sufficient data support.
- Instruction Optimization Suggestions:
  1. "Bottleneck descriptions should be detailed and specific."
  2. "Quantify delay times."
  3. "List breakdowns of cost components."
  4. "Improvement measures should be concrete and actionable."
  5. "The division of responsibilities is clear without a doubt."
  6. "It is recommended to use terms like 'process reengineering standards.'"
  7. "The chart presentation is intuitive and clear."
  8. "Data references must be accurate."
  9. "The expression must be logically rigorous."
  10. "Include explanations for key nodes."
  11. "Use terms like 'cost-benefit analysis.'"
  12. "The structure of the plan is well-organized."
  13. "It is recommended to use keywords like 'quantitative comparison.'"
  14. "Emphasize cost reduction and efficiency improvement."
  15. "Add 'resource integration' to optimize the wording."
  16. "The expression should be concise and clear."
  17. "It is recommended to use terms like 'strong operability.'"
  18. "Emphasize the continuous improvement mechanism."
  19. "Data support is comprehensive and thorough."
  20. "Use terms like 'standardized process.'"

## Case 14: Real Estate – Property Management Improvement Plan Writing

- Scenario Description:
  A real estate company aims to improve property service quality and reduce complaints while increasing customer satisfaction. They need to create a property management improvement plan.
- Detailed Steps:
  1. Initial generation: Input instructions. "Please generate a draft of the 'Property Management Improvement Plan', which should include current situation analysis, existing problems, improvement measures, expected effects, and future plans. The language should be formal and the structure clear."
  2. First presentation: The "current situation analysis" section lacks data.
  3. Feedback for revision: Additional instructions.
     "Please add property complaint data and customer satisfaction statistics in the 'current situation analysis' section, and include specific improvement Detailed Steps and responsibility division in the 'improvement measures' section."
  4. Multiple rounds of feedback: Suggest adding a technology upgrade plan in the "future plans" section.
  5. Final output: A comprehensive, data-rich, and detailed property management improvement plan is generated.
- Instruction Optimization Suggestions:
  Optimization suggestions for instructions:
  1. "The current situation data must be detailed and accurate."
  2. "Complaints statistics should be presented in a quantifiable manner."
  3. "Satisfaction data must be precise."
  4. "Improvement measures should be specific and clear."
  5. "The division of responsibilities should be clear and defined."
  6. "It is recommended to use keywords like 'process reengineering.'"
  7. "The format should be standardized and uniform."
  8. "The language should be objective and rigorous."
  9. "Third-party test data should be referenced."
  10. "Include a technology upgrade plan."
  11. "Emphasize service quality improvement."
  12. "Use phrases like 'data-driven improvement.'"
  13. "Include customer feedback examples."
  14. "Use keywords like 'standardized management.'"
  15. "Detail the operation Detailed Steps."
  16. "Ensure the logical structure is clear and organized."
  17. "Emphasize continuous monitoring."
  18. "Add 'significant benefits' to the wording."

19. "It is recommended to use phrases like 'risk early warning mechanism.'"
20. "Use phrases like 'clear improvement goals.'"

## Case 15: Automotive – New Model Promotion Copywriting

- Scenario Description:
  An automotive manufacturing company is about to launch a brand-new smart electric SUV. The marketing department needs to write an eye-catching promotional copy to capture the market.
- Detailed Steps:
  1. Initial generation: Input instructions. "Please generate a draft promotional copy for the 'Brand-new Smart Electric SUV', which should include product highlights, technical advantages, market positioning, and user experience descriptions. The language should be concise and powerful."
  2. First presentation: The "product highlights" section is not vivid enough.
  3. Feedback for revision: Additional instructions.
     "Please add specific technical parameters and real user feedback examples in the 'product highlights' section, using metaphors to enhance emotional expression."
  4. Multiple rounds of feedback: The user requests a more modern and technological style for the overall copy.
  5. Final output: A lively, data-rich, and engaging promotional copy is generated.
- Optimization Suggestions for Instructions:
  1. "The product highlights should be vivid and specific."
  2. "Technical parameters should be described in detail."
  3. "Real user feedback data should be referenced."
  4. "It is recommended to use metaphors to enhance the expression."
  5. "The tone should have a modern and technological feel."
  6. "The title should be eye-catching."
  7. "The copy should be concise and powerful."
  8. "Emphasize the brand's unique selling points."
  9. "The expression should be lively and attention-grabbing."
  10. "Include details on high-end configurations."
  11. "It is recommended to use descriptions like 'leading technology.'"
  12. "Data references must be accurate."
  13. "The logical structure should be clear and rigorous."
  14. "The details should be specific and rich."
  15. "Emphasize quality assurance."
  16. "Use popular terms to enhance relatability."
  17. "Adjust the writing style to balance the expression."

18. "The wording should be clear and direct."
19. "It is recommended to include keywords like 'futuristic' and 'intelligent.'"
20. "Emphasize 'eye-catching', 'innovative', and 'fashionable.'"

## Case 16: Logistics – Logistics Process Optimization Plan Writing

– Scenario Description:
  A logistics company is facing issues with delivery delays and rising costs. There is an urgent need to create a logistics process optimization plan to improve overall operational efficiency.
– Detailed Steps:
  1. Initial generation: Input instructions. "Please generate a draft of the 'Logistics Process Optimization Plan,' which should include the current logistics process, bottleneck analysis, optimization measures, and expected benefits. The language should be standard and the data should be detailed."
  2. First presentation: The "bottleneck analysis" section lacks specificity.
  3. Feedback for revision: Additional instructions.
     "Please add detailed data on delay times and transportation costs in the 'bottleneck analysis' section, and clarify the responsible departments and execution timelines in the optimization measures."
  4. Multiple rounds of feedback: Suggest adding quantitative metrics in the "expected benefits" section.
  5. Final output: Generate a logistics process optimization plan with a clear structure and sufficient data support.
– Instruction Optimization Suggestions:
  1. "The bottleneck description must be specific and detailed."
  2. "Delay times should be explained in quantitative terms."
  3. "Transportation costs should be broken down into subcategories."
  4. "Improvement measures need to be actionable."
  5. "The responsible departments must have clear divisions of labor."
  6. "The time nodes should be precisely defined."
  7. "It is recommended to use expressions like 'process reengineering standards.'"
  8. "Data and charts should be presented in an intuitive manner."
  9. "The copy should have rigorous logical expression."
  10. "Emphasize cost reduction and efficiency improvement goals."
  11. "Use phrases like 'Key Performance Indicators' (KPIs)."
  12. "Include a resource integration explanation."
  13. "Adopt a bullet-point structure."
  14. "Data references must be accurate."
  15. "It is recommended to use descriptions of standard processes."
  16. "Emphasize a continuous improvement mechanism."

17. "The expression should be concise and clear."
18. "Use terms related to cost reduction and efficiency improvement."
19. "Add terms like 'key nodes' and 'benefit improvement' to optimize the wording."
20. "Emphasize standardization of operational processes."

## Case 17: IT Software Services – Project Requirements Document Writing

- Scenario:
  A certain IT company plans to develop an enterprise management system and needs to write a detailed project requirements document to clarify various functions and technical specifications.
- Detailed Steps:
  1. Initial generation: Input instructions.
     "Please generate a draft of the 'New Enterprise Management System Requirements Document,' which should include functional requirements, system architecture, technical specifications, and user scenario descriptions. The language should be professional and the structure clear."
  2. First presentation: The "technical specifications" section lacks detail.
  3. Feedback for revision: Additional instructions.
     "Please add specific performance parameters and security requirements in the 'technical specifications' section, and include real case examples in the 'user scenarios' section."
  4. Multiple rounds of feedback: Suggest further refinement of functional requirements.
  5. Final output: A comprehensive and detailed project requirements document with a complete structure is generated.
- Instruction Optimization Suggestions:
  1. "Functional requirements should be detailed and clear."
  2. "Technical specifications should be quantified and specific."
  3. "Security requirements should be professional and rigorous."
  4. "User scenarios should be closely aligned with real situations."
  5. "Data parameters should be referenced accurately."
  6. "The structure should have clear hierarchical organization."
  7. "Use professional terminology for explanations."
  8. "Include scalability explanations."
  9. "Format should be standardized and uniform."
  10. "It is recommended to use requirement refinement techniques."
  11. "Provide risk alerts."
  12. "Emphasize the overall system architecture."

13. "Use bullet points for clear expression."
14. "It is recommended to reference market research data."
15. "Emphasize clear development goals."
16. "Include interface design explanations."
17. "Use functional module divisions."
18. "Wording should be concise and clear."
19. "Include terms like 'detailed parameters,' 'technical standards.'"
20. "Emphasize user feedback and adjustments."

## Case 18: Cultural Media – Corporate Promotional Video Script Writing

- Scenario Description:
  A cultural media company plans to produce a promotional video to enhance the corporate brand image and needs to write an engaging script.
- Detailed Steps:
  1. Initial generation: Input instructions.
     "Please generate a draft script for the promotional video on 'Corporate Digital Transformation,' which should include the opening, brand story, core values, and a closing call-to-action. The language should be compelling."
  2. First presentation: The "brand story" section is too bland.
  3. Feedback for revision: Additional instructions.
     "Please add specific cases and touching metaphors in the 'brand story' section, and use a more motivational tone."
  4. Multiple rounds of feedback: Request for a more motivational tone throughout the script.
  5. Final output: A script with rich content, sincere emotions, and a complete structure is generated.
- Instruction Optimization Suggestions:
  1. "The brand story should be emotionally engaging."
  2. "Case descriptions should be specific and vivid."
  3. "Use vivid metaphors to enhance emotional appeal."
  4. "The tone should be strong and inspiring."
  5. "The language should have a sense of imagery."
  6. "It is recommended to use emotional resonance vocabulary."
  7. "Add phrases like 'strong narrative.'"
  8. "Emphasize the core values of the brand."
  9. "The structure should have clear segments."
  10. "It is recommended to use action verbs to enhance the tone."
  11. "Data references should be precise."
  12. "Incorporate visual effects descriptions."

13. "Use interactive calls to action."
14. "Ensure the script maintains consistency between sections."
15. "It is recommended to add an inspiring ending."
16. "Expression should be straightforward and easy to understand."
17. "Use a passionate tone."
18. "It is recommended to reference successful cases."
19. "Emphasize innovative expression methods."
20. "Use keywords like 'passion,' 'moving,' 'inspiring,' 'sincere.'"

## Case 19: Hotel Management – Customer Satisfaction Survey Report Writing

- Scenario Description:
  A chain hotel wishes to improve service quality and needs to write a customer satisfaction survey report to identify problems and propose improvement plans through data analysis.
- Detailed Steps:
  1. Initial generation: Input instructions. "Please generate a draft of the 'Customer Satisfaction Survey Report,' which should include the survey background, data analysis, main issues, and improvement suggestions. The language should be objective, and the data should be detailed."
  2. First presentation: The "data analysis" section lacks chart support.
  3. Feedback for revision: Additional instructions.
     "Please add bar charts and pie charts in the 'data analysis' section to show customer satisfaction data and issue distribution."
  4. Multiple rounds of feedback: Suggest including specific service improvement cases in the "improvement suggestions" section.
  5. Final output: A well-structured, data-rich report with visual elements is generated.
- Instruction Optimization Suggestions:
  1. "Data analysis should be detailed and intuitive."
  2. "Charts must be clear."
  3. "It is recommended to use professional statistical terminology."
  4. "Improvement suggestions should be specific and clear."
  5. "Customer feedback should reference real cases."
  6. "Data sources must be accurate."
  7. "The format should be standardized."
  8. "Language should be objective and professional."
  9. "Include quantitative analysis."
  10. "Use trend graphs for assistance."
  11. "Structure should be well-organized."

12. “It is recommended to use comparative data analysis.”
13. “Emphasize service optimization measures.”
14. “Use phrases like ‘detailed survey.’”
15. “The expression should be concise and powerful.”
16. “Include customer experience feedback.”
17. “Use terms like ‘regression analysis.’”
18. “Emphasize data-supported decision-making.”
19. “Include expert recommendations.”
20. “Optimize the wording by adding ‘objective,’ ‘rigorous,’ ‘detailed,’ and ‘precise.’”

## Case 20: Sports and Fitness – Corporate Fitness Promotion Plan Generation

- Scenario:
  A large company plans to develop an internal fitness promotion plan to improve employees’ health levels and encourage participation in fitness activities.
- Detailed Steps:
  1. Initial generation: Input instructions. “Please generate a draft of the ‘Corporate Fitness Promotion Plan,’ which should include the promotion background, activity arrangements, implementation Detailed Steps, and expected effects. The language should be concise, and the data should be well-supported.”
  2. First presentation: The “activity arrangements” section is too vague.
  3. Feedback for revision: Additional instructions. “Please list the time, location, participation methods, and incentive mechanisms for each fitness activity in the ‘activity arrangements’ section, and add quantitative indicators in the expected effects.”
  4. Multiple rounds of feedback: Request for the plan to be more actionable overall.
  5. Final output: A fitness promotion plan with a clear structure, specific measures, and clear data is generated.
- Instruction Optimization Suggestions:
  1. “The activity arrangements should be specific and detailed.”
  2. “Time and location must be clearly defined.”
  3. “Participation methods should be clearly described.”
  4. “Incentive mechanisms should be expressed quantitatively.”
  5. “Expected effects should be well-supported by data.”
  6. “The plan structure should be logically organized.”
  7. “It is recommended to use expressions like ‘health indicator improvement.’”
  8. “The language should be friendly and clear.”
  9. “Adjust the tone to be positive and inspiring.”

10. "Include an employee feedback mechanism."
11. "It is recommended to use real data for support."
12. "The expression should be concise and powerful."
13. "Emphasize the continuous improvement plan."
14. "Use phrases like 'regular evaluation mechanism.'"
15. "Include a health training plan."
16. "It is recommended to include incentive and reward mechanisms."
17. "Emphasize 'strong operability.'"
18. "The structure should have clear bullet points."
19. "Data references must be accurate."
20. "Optimize wording by adding 'practical,' 'forward-looking,' 'healthy,' and 'innovative.'"

## Case 21: Agricultural Technology – Smart Agriculture Promotion Plan Generation

- Scenario:
  An agricultural technology company needs to create a smart agriculture promotion plan to improve farmers' production efficiency and product quality by promoting its smart agricultural equipment.
- Detailed Steps:
  1. Initial generation: Input instructions. "Please generate a draft of the 'Smart Agriculture Promotion Plan' that should include product introduction, application cases, market prospects, and promotion strategies. The language should be standardized and the data should be detailed."
  2. First presentation: The "application cases" section is insufficient.
  3. Feedback for revision: Additional instructions.
     "Please add actual usage data and farmer feedback in the 'application cases' section, and include competitor analysis in the 'market prospects' section."
  4. Multiple rounds of feedback: Suggest adding specific Detailed Steps in the "promotion strategies" section.
  5. Final output: Generate a detailed, data-rich, and clear smart agriculture promotion plan.
- Instruction Optimization Suggestions:
  1. "Product introduction must be detailed."
  2. "Application cases should be real and specific."
  3. "Farmer feedback should be quantified."
  4. "Market prospects should be well-supported with data."
  5. "Competitor analysis should be detailed and accurate."
  6. "Promotion strategies should be actionable."

7. "It is recommended to use terms like 'smart agriculture' and 'digital agriculture.'"
8. "Language expression should be professional and objective."
9. "Format should be standardized and uniform."
10. "Include actual usage effects."
11. "Data references must be accurate."
12. "The expression should have a clear structure."
13. "Use phrases like 'technological innovation' and 'benefit enhancement.'"
14. "Ensure the promotion process is clear."
15. "Optimize wording by adding 'positive feedback' and 'market expansion.'"
16. "Emphasize significant benefits."
17. "Use practical cases to support the plan."
18. "It is recommended to include future outlook predictions."
19. "Expression should be logically rigorous."
20. "Use terms like 'data-driven' and 'high practical value.' '述.'"

## Case 22: Environmental Protection Industry – Green Project Application Report Generation

- Scenario:
  An environmental protection company plans to apply for government support funding and needs to write a green project application report, focusing on demonstrating the project's contribution to environmental improvement.
- Detailed Steps:
  1. Initial generation: Input instructions. "Please generate a draft of the 'Green Project Application Report,' which should include project background, environmental benefits, technical solutions, and funding requirements. The language should be formal, and the data should be detailed."
  2. First presentation: The "environmental benefits" section is too vague.
  3. Feedback for revision: Additional instructions.
     "Please add specific data and comparative analysis in the 'environmental benefits' section, explain the project's specific contribution to pollution reduction, and describe the technical solutions in detail."
  4. Multiple rounds of feedback: Request to supplement details of the funding requirements.
  5. Final output: Generate a green project application report with a complete structure, sufficient data, and strong persuasiveness.
- Instruction Optimization Suggestions:
  1. "Environmental benefits data should be sufficient."
  2. "Comparative analysis should be intuitively presented."
  3. "Technical solutions should be detailed and specific."

4. "Funding requirements should be quantified and clear."
5. "The structure should be rigorous and complete."
6. "Language should be formal and professional."
7. "It is recommended to use keywords such as 'green development indicators.'"
8. "Reference policy documents."
9. "Data charts should be standardized and clear."
10. "Optimize wording by adding 'significant environmental benefits.'"
11. "Emphasize sustainable development."
12. "Use terms like 'ecological restoration' and 'pollution control.'"
13. "The logic of expression should be clear."
14. "Include project risk assessments."
15. "It is recommended to add economic benefit analysis."
16. "Use case comparisons."
17. "The wording should be concise and powerful."
18. "Emphasize environmental standardization."
19. "It is recommended to use terms like 'data comparison' and 'empirical analysis.'"
20. "Optimize wording by adding 'standardized,' 'innovative,' and 'practical.'"

## Case 23: Air Transport – Aviation Safety Report Generation

- Scenario Description:
  An airline company needs to write an aviation safety operations report to improve operational safety, recording in detail the safety incidents and improvement measures of the past year.
- Detailed Steps:
  1. Initial generation: Input instructions. "Please generate a draft of the 'Aviation Safety Operations Report,' which should include safety status, existing risks, improvement measures, and future planning. The language should be formal, and the data should be detailed."
  2. First presentation: The "existing risks" section lacks specific cases.
  3. Feedback for revision: Additional instructions.
     "Please add safety incident data and actual cases from the past year in the 'existing risks' section, and clarify the division of responsibilities in the 'improvement measures' section."
  4. Multiple rounds of feedback: Request to include goals and timelines in the "future planning" section.
  5. Final output: Generate a data-rich aviation safety report with specific cases and clear improvement measures.

- Instruction Optimization Suggestions:
  1. "Safety risk descriptions must be specific."
  2. "Support with actual cases."
  3. "Data statistics should be detailed and accurate."
  4. "Improvement measures should be clear and specific."
  5. "Responsibilities should be clearly divided."
  6. "It is recommended to use terms like 'accident rate reduction indicators.'"
  7. "Format requirements should be strictly standardized."
  8. "Language should be professional and rigorous."
  9. "Include a risk early warning mechanism."
  10. "It is recommended to add safety management standards."
  11. "Expression should be logically rigorous."
  12. "It is recommended to include an improvement timeline."
  13. "Emphasize data-driven approaches."
  14. "It is recommended to use safety improvement plans."
  15. "Wording should be concise and effective."
  16. "Add keywords such as 'responsibility tracking.'"
  17. "Include historical data comparisons."
  18. "Add detailed accident case studies."
  19. "Focus on operational feasibility of improvements."
  20. "Use expressions like 'standardized safety procedures.'"

## Case 24: Energy – New Energy Investment Research Report Generation

- Scenario Description:
  A new energy enterprise needs to write a new energy investment Research Report to evaluate market prospects and investment risks, focusing on policy impacts and the competitive landscape.
- Detailed Steps:
  1. Initial generation: Input instructions.
     "Please generate a draft of the 'New Energy Investment Research Report,' which should include market status, competitive landscape, policy impacts, and investment recommendations. The language should be objective, and the data should be detailed."
  2. First presentation: The "policy impacts" section is not in-depth enough.
  3. Feedback for revision: Additional instructions.
     "Please add specific policy provisions and market impact analysis in the 'policy impacts' section, and supplement risk alerts in the 'investment recommendations' section."
  4. Multiple rounds of feedback: Suggest adding competitor data comparisons.

5. Final output: Generate a complete, data-rich investment Research Report with clear risk alerts.

- Instruction Optimization Suggestions:
  1. "Policy analysis should be in-depth and detailed."
  2. "Market competition data comparisons should be clear."
  3. "Investment recommendations should include sufficient risk alerts."
  4. "Format should include both text and visuals."
  5. "It is recommended to use quantitative analysis methods."
  6. "Expression should be logically clear."
  7. "Data references must be accurate."
  8. "Include industry standard data."
  9. "Emphasize forward-looking market forecasts."
  10. "Use professional financial terminology."
  11. "Optimize wording by adding 'stable' and 'scientific.'"
  12. "Emphasize data-driven decision-making."
  13. "Use charts to aid explanations."
  14. "It is recommended to add risk control models."
  15. "Wording should be concise and powerful."
  16. "Include detailed competitor analysis."
  17. "Emphasize investment portfolio optimization."
  18. "It is recommended to add strategic planning."
  19. "Expression should be forward-looking yet rigorous."
  20. "Use expressions like 'dynamic adjustment' and 'market volatility.'"

## Case 25: Telecommunications – 5G Application Promotion Report Generation

- Scenario Description:
  A telecommunications enterprise plans to promote its newly developed 5G technology applications and needs to write a detailed report introducing technical advantages, real application cases, and future market forecasts.
- Detailed Steps:
  1. Initial generation: Input instructions.
     "Please generate a draft of the '5G Application Promotion Report,' which should include technical advantages, market status, real application cases, and future trend forecasts. The language should be standardized, and the data should be detailed."
  2. First presentation: The "real application cases" section is not specific enough.

3. Feedback for revision: Additional instructions.
   "Please add specific customer use cases and feedback data in the 'real application cases' section, and provide detailed market forecasts in the 'future trend forecasts' section."
4. Multiple rounds of feedback: Request for the overall style of the report to be more forward-looking.
5. Final output: Generate a detailed, forward-looking, and data-supported 5G application promotion report.

- Instruction Optimization Suggestions:
  1. "Application cases must be specific and detailed."
  2. Provide quantitative descriptions of customer feedback.
  3. Ensure market forecasts are detailed and forward-looking.
  4. Sufficient data support is required.
  5. The structure should be logically rigorous.
  6. Use professional yet concise language.
  7. Suggested use of keywords such as "5G Revolution" and "Technological Leadership."
  8. Include dynamic market analysis.
  9. Emphasize specific user experiences.
  10. Recommend citing authoritative industry data.
  11. Ensure the format is rich in both text and visuals.
  12. Incorporate keywords like "Innovation" and "Cutting-edge."
  13. Expression should be clear and standardized.
  14. Suggest adding practical application details.
  15. Highlight market expansion strategies.
  16. Focus on competitive comparative analysis.
  17. Recommend using trend forecasting models.
  18. The writing must maintain clear logical flow.
  19. Include keywords like "Foresight" and "Technological Breakthroughs."
  20. Emphasize strategic planning.

## Case 26: Public Utilities – City Water Supply Annual Report Generation

- Scenario:
  A city water supply company needs to write an annual report to evaluate the stability and safety of the water supply, guiding future facility upgrades and maintenance plans.

- Detailed Steps:
  1. Initial generation: Input instructions.
     "Please generate a draft of the 'City Water Supply Annual Report' which should include water supply status, water supply safety, existing issues, improvement measures, and future plans. The language should be objective, and the data should be detailed."
  2. First presentation: The "water supply safety" section lacks specific data support.
  3. Feedback for revision: Additional instructions.
     "Please add accident statistics and safety hazard analysis in the 'water supply safety' section, and clarify responsible departments and the technical upgrade plan in the 'improvement measures' section."
  4. Multiple rounds of feedback: Request to add technical upgrade goals in the 'future plans' section.
  5. Final output: Generate a city water supply annual report with a clear structure and sufficient data.
- Instruction Optimization Suggestions:
  1. "The water supply status description must be detailed."
  2. "Safety data should be quantified accurately."
  3. "Accident statistics should be specific and comprehensive."
  4. "Improvement measures must be actionable."
  5. "The division of responsibilities should be clear and detailed."
  6. "The technical upgrade plan should be forward-looking."
  7. "It is recommended to use data charts for intuitive presentation."
  8. "The expression should be objective and rigorous."
  9. "Include a safety monitoring mechanism."
  10. "Emphasize the continuous improvement goals."
  11. "Use phrases like 'standardized testing.'"
  12. "It is recommended to reference third-party reports."
  13. "The wording should be concise and clear."
  14. "Include long-term planning indicators."
  15. "Data support must be comprehensive."
  16. "Format requirements should be uniform and standardized."
  17. "It is recommended to use a risk early warning system."
  18. "Optimize wording by adding 'comprehensive analysis.'"
  19. "Emphasize clear improvement goals."
  20. "Use terms like 'standard', 'scientific', and 'systematic.'"

## Case 27: Government Procurement – Procurement Project Request Writing

- Scenario Description:
  A government department plans to procure efficient equipment. To ensure the process is standardized and the budget is reasonable, a procurement project request needs to be written, detailing the procurement requirements and expected benefits.
- Detailed Steps:
  1. Initial generation: Input instructions.
     "Please generate a draft of the 'Procurement Project Request' which should include procurement requirements, equipment parameters, budget plan, and expected benefits. The language should be formal and the data should be detailed."
  2. First presentation: The "procurement requirements" section lacks clarity.
  3. Feedback for revision: Additional instructions.
     "Please add a detailed description in the 'procurement requirements' section, including usage scenarios and technical requirements, and list specific numbers and cost breakdowns in the 'budget plan.'"
  4. Multiple rounds of feedback: Request to add comparative data and success cases in the "expected benefits" section.
  5. Final output: A procurement project request draft with clear content, sufficient data, and rigorous logic is generated.
- Instruction Optimization Suggestions:
  1. "Procurement requirements should be detailed and clear."
  2. "Usage scenarios should be specifically described."
  3. "Technical requirements should be professional and accurate."
  4. "The budget plan should be quantified and detailed."
  5. "Data references must be accurate."
  6. "The format should be standardized and compliant."
  7. "It is recommended to use a cost breakdown explanation."
  8. "Include expressions like 'quantified expected benefits.'"
  9. "Emphasize the risk early warning mechanism."
  10. "The expression should be logical and organized."
  11. "Use phrases like 'clear responsibilities.'"
  12. "Add historical data comparison."
  13. "Reference successful cases."
  14. "It is recommended to use phrases like 'transparent budget.'"
  15. "The wording should be concise and powerful."
  16. "Emphasize the standardization of the procurement process."
  17. "Use phrases like 'cost control.'"
  18. "Include implementation details."

19. "It is recommended to clearly define the approval process."
20. "Optimize the wording by adding 'specific numbers,' 'clear requirements,' and 'detailed breakdowns.'"

## Case 28: Technology R&D – Project Proposal Draft Generation

- Scenario Description:
  A technology R&D institution plans to apply for funding for a new enterprise management system project and needs to write a project proposal to secure R&D support.
- Detailed Steps:
  1. Initial generation: Input instruction.
     "Please generate a draft of a Technology Project Proposal, including project background, research objectives, technical approach, budget plan, and expected outcomes. The language should be concise and clear, with accurate and detailed data."
  2. First output: The "Technical Approach" section is too brief.
  3. Feedback & revision: Add instruction: "Please expand the 'Technical Approach' section with specific experimental methods, key technical indicators, and expected breakthroughs. Also, in the 'Budget Plan' section, list each cost item in detail."
  4. Multiple rounds of feedback: Request to add quantitative indicators in the "Expected Outcomes" section.
  5. Final output: A well-structured, detailed, and highly actionable project proposal.
- Instruction Optimization Suggestions:
  1. "Technical approach must be detailed and specific."
  2. "Experimental methods should be clear."
  3. "Key technical indicators must be quantified."
  4. "Budget plan should be data-rich."
  5. "Project background should be comprehensive."
  6. "Research objectives should be clear and specific."
  7. "Proposal structure should be well-organized."
  8. "Include a risk assessment section."
  9. "Add phased goals."
  10. "Emphasize reasonable R&D investment."
  11. "Ensure all data citations are accurate."
  12. "Include standardization requirements."
  13. "Highlight innovation and feasibility."
  14. "Use detailed bullet points."
  15. "Maintain professional and rigorous language."

16. "Include keywords such as 'experimental design' and 'technical breakthrough.'"
17. "Add market outlook forecasts."
18. "Attach a detailed appendix."
19. "Include comprehensive evaluation metrics."
20. "Emphasize practicality and completeness."

## Case 29: Supply Chain Management – Logistics Cost Research Report Writing

- Scenario Description:
  A supply chain management company seeks to lower overall transportation costs and needs to write a logistics cost Research Report to break down cost components and propose optimization measures.
- Detailed Steps:
  1. Initial generation: Input instruction: "Please generate a draft of a Logistics Cost Research Report, including cost breakdown, data analysis, existing problems, and optimization recommendations. The language should be formal, with comprehensive and accurate data."
  2. First output: The "Cost Breakdown" section is insufficiently detailed.
  3. Feedback & revision: Add instruction: "Please break down each cost item in detail in the 'Cost Breakdown' section and include charts showing each category's proportion. Also, in the 'Optimization Recommendations' section, propose specific measures for cost reduction."
  4. Multiple rounds of feedback: Request to add historical comparison data in the "Data Analysis" section.
  5. Final output: A clear, data-rich logistics cost Research Report with specific and actionable optimization measures.
- Instruction Optimization Suggestions:
  1. "Cost breakdown should be clearly categorized."
  2. "Charts should be intuitive and clear."
  3. "Data analysis should include detailed comparisons."
  4. "Optimization measures should be specific and practical."
  5. "Clarify responsibilities."
  6. "Include cost control indicators."
  7. "Maintain standardized formatting."
  8. "Language should be concise and powerful."
  9. "Add historical data comparisons."
  10. "Emphasize continuous improvement mechanisms."
  11. "Use quantitative analysis methods."
  12. "Include resource integration plans."

13. "Maintain logical and orderly structure."
14. "Include terms like 'economical and practical.'"
15. "Ensure data accuracy."
16. "Use cost breakdown charts."
17. "Highlight the goal of 'improving efficiency.'"
18. "Keep expressions clear and structured."
19. "Add real-world case studies."
20. "Use keywords like 'cost reduction and efficiency improvement' and 'data-driven.'"

## Case 30: Health and Wellness – Corporate Health Management Plan Generation

- Scenario Description:
  A large enterprise aims to improve employee health and reduce medical expenses by creating a detailed corporate health management plan covering current health status, improvement measures, and expected outcomes.
- Detailed Steps:
  1. Initial generation: Input instruction: "Please generate a draft of a Corporate Health Management Plan, including current health status, existing issues, improvement measures, and expected outcomes. The language should be formal, with accurate and detailed data."
  2. First output: The "Improvement Measures" section is too general.
  3. Feedback and revision: Add instruction: "Please specify health improvement plans, employee training programs, and monitoring indicators in the 'Improvement Measures' section. In the 'Expected Outcomes' section, quantify the projected improvements in health data."
  4. Multiple rounds of feedback: Request more rigorous overall logic and richer details.
  5. Final output: A well-structured, concrete, and data-driven corporate health management plan.
- Instruction Optimization Suggestions:
  1. "Provide comprehensive health status data."
  2. "Improvement measures should be specific and actionable."
  3. "Detail the training program."
  4. "Quantify monitoring indicators."
  5. "Support expected outcomes with sufficient data."
  6. "Include regular health assessments."
  7. "Keep plan structure well-organized."
  8. "Use expressions like 'data-driven decision-making.'"
  9. "Include phrases like 'improve health indicators.'"

10. “Language should be professional yet approachable.”
11. “Include keywords such as ‘continuous improvement.’”
12. “Use terms like ‘employee health promotion.’”
13. “Ensure data accuracy.”
14. “Plan should be comprehensive and systematic.”
15. “Emphasize long-term planning.”
16. “Add a feedback mechanism for results.”
17. “Keep expressions concise and impactful.”
18. “Include practical examples.”
19. “Incorporate health management standards.”
20. “Emphasize clarity, foresight, and professionalism.”

# Index



 | https://doi.org/10.1515/9783112218181-013

www.ingramcontent.com/pod-product-compliance
Lightning Source LLC
LaVergne TN
LVHW081319110826
845149LV00006B/1546
*9783119143899*